**Publisher 's Acknowledgments**

We're proud of this book and the people who worked on it. For details on how to create your own book visit us online.

 Some of the people who helped bring this book to market include the Following

: **Project Editor** Thia T Nguyen     **Graphic Designer** Gregory Spencer

## *DEDICATION*

Dedicated to the many friends, family and customers who have supported me for 15 years of business.

Also dedicated to Eldora Kenan, my Granny.

# TABLE OF CONTENTS

*"People don't realize how a man's whole life can be changed by one book."*

-Malcom                                     X

# INTRODUCTION

This is an inspiration guide to running, starting, operating and managing your new business. Everyone has a dream of starting their own business. Many wishful thinkers wonder where to start, how do I start, and how much will it cost.

Will people support you spending their money?

These are some of the questions you find yourself asking.

My advice to anyone wanting to start a business, make sure you are able to sacrifice and see through the long hall. So, you woke up ready to become a business owner. You realized that you have a product or service people will pay for. "I am ready.", you said. "Let's do this!!", So what do I need to do first to get started?

You have figured out your passion but are you ready to be a business owner?

Do you need good credit?

Do you need a lot of money or a loan?

Make sure you do your research and homework before you start.

# How This Book Is Arranged

*Let's faces facts: As a small business owner or leader you don't have lots of time to waste. You want to get the information you need quickly so you can make a decision and get back to business. I understand that, so I have broken down several key things into small chapters that get right to the point.*

*If you don't have time to read every book and search the internet that's fine. Simply keep this book handy and brush through the chapters for immediate quick references. If you have just started or wanting to start your mall business. You can skip around and read as you need and come back later to different chapters but will list several important things you don't want to miss.*

**This way of money making is riskier but more straightforward than working a job. There is no boss to decide what happens to you.**

**There are 4 protagonists: you, your customers, your investors, and your co-founder. If you succeed, they succeed. And the way to making money for you looks like this:**

1. Find a product (or idea) that is popular but not yet perfect
2. Buy one and study it in detail
3. Figure out how to improve it
4. Make a prototype
5. Show the prototype to 100 people
6. Remake it until people are willing to pre-order (for example on Kickstarter)
7. Find a co-founder who can build it with you
8. **Split the equity** – give your co-founder 50%, but use a vesting agreement so that their share becomes worth more the longer they work on the company
9. Find an investor. This can be a person who has a lot of money (an angel investor)
10. Give her or him 10% of your company
11. Make the product Sell your product to 1 Million people Get more money (this time from VCs)
12. List your company on stock exchange (this is after you've either raised a lot of money or have a lot of revenue, or better yet profit)
13. Sell a lot of shares when you list on stock exchange
14. Then just wait out the cooling off period (about 6 months) and you will have your money

# CHAPTER 1

## Advantages of Small-Business Ownership

**Independence.** Entrepreneurs are their own bosses. They make the decisions. They choose whom to do business with and what work they will do. They decide what hours to work, as well as what to pay and whether to take vacations. For many entrepreneurs the freedom to control their destiny is enough to outweigh the potential risks.

**Financial gain.** Entrepreneurship offers a greater possibility of achieving significant financial rewards than working for someone else. Owning your own business removes the income restraint that exists in being someone else's employee. Many entrepreneurs are inspired by the mega-millionaire entrepreneurs we see today.

**Control.** It enables one to be involved in the total operation of the business, from concept to design to creation, from sales to business operations to customer response. This ability to be totally immersed in the business is very satisfying to entrepreneurs who are driven by passion and creativity and possess a "vision" of what they aim to achieve. This level of involvement allows the business owner to truly create something of their own.

**Prestige.** It offers the status of being the person in charge. Some entrepreneurs are attracted to the idea of being the boss. In addition, though, there is the prestige and pride of ownership. When someone asks, "Who did this?" the entrepreneur can answer, "I did."

**Equity.** It gives an individual the opportunity to build equity, which can be kept, sold, or passed on to the next generation. It's not uncommon for entrepreneurs to own multiple businesses throughout their life. They establish a company, run it for a while, and later sell it to someone else. The income from this sale can then be used to finance the next venture. If they're not interested in selling the business, the goal may be to build something that can be passed down to their children to help ensure their financial future. One thing is sure: In order to fully reap the financial benefits of a business venture, you need to be the owner.

**Opportunity.** Entrepreneurship creates an opportunity for a person to make a contribution. Most new entrepreneurs help the local economy. A few—through their innovations—contribute to society

## Cons of Starting a Business

## *No guaranteed salary or paycheck.

There is always a financial risk involved in starting a business. You may not make money for some period of time. You may have to put your own money into the business. Depending on your business you may not get a check for a while. It is said that takes about 3 to 5 years to actually see a profit after all the expenses.

## It's all on you.

Feels good to be the boss when times are good. In other words, along with making exciting and fun decisions like who are to hold the grand opening party you have some big decisions to make.

## You can't please everyone.

When you work for someone else you may be able to excel in the art of making your boss happier even happy with your performance.

As the boss, however there will be occasions you won't be able to make everyone or even anyone happy and will have to make some hard choices in the best interest of the business

# Think like a Businessperson

If you're going to be an entrepreneur, you need to think like one daily. First you need to see yourself as a people person. You will need to be able to establish and maintain many relationships in a professional business manner, including those with suppliers, customers, investors and the bank. You must think of yourself as a leader and be able to lead and manage employees. You will need to be able to communicate effectively with a variety of personality types. Be able to present yourself and your business in a short version. When you first start your business will be 24/7. Even during non-business hours, you will focus on aspect of your business and constantly be thinking of ways it can be improved.

### Don't cut the Wrong corners

While you don't want to spend money foolishly, you need to carefully determine where to save and where to spend money. Spending a fortune to create a product, then trying to save money by not having and advertising or marketing campaign is a waste of your efforts. You have to live with the decision of your business and brand the only thing differs is your determination to be successful.

*Ultimately, it is up to you to determine which type of entity is best for your current needs and future business goals.*

**1. Know yourself, your true motivational level,** the amount of money you can risk, and what you're willing to do to be successful. Sure, we all want to make millions of dollars. But what are you willing to give up reaching that goal? How many hours a week will you work on an ongoing basis? How far out of your comfort zone are you willing to stretch?
How far will your family stretch with you? To be successful, keep your business plans in line with your personal and family goals and resources.

**2. Choose the right business for you.** The old formula – find a need and fill it – still works. It will always work. The key to success is finding needs that you can fill, that you want to fill, and that will produce enough income to build a profitable business.

**3.Be sure there really is a market for what you want to sell.** One of the biggest mistake's startups make is to assume a lot of people will want to buy a particular product or service, because the business owner likes the ideas or knows one or two people who want the product or service. To minimize your risk for loss, never assume there is a market. Research the idea. Talk to real potential prospects (who aren't family and friends) to find out if what you want to sell is something they'd be interested in buying, and if so, what they'd pay for the product or service.

**4.Plan to succeed.** If you're not seeking investors or putting a huge sum of money into your business, you may not need an elaborate business plan, but you still do need a plan - one that specifies your goal – your destination – and then lays out at least a skeletal road map for how you'll get to where you want to go. The plan will change as you progress and learn more about your customers and competition, but it will still help you stay focused and headed in the right directions. Use our business planning worksheet to help develop that basic plan.

**5.Don't procrastinate.** I've heard some people advise would-be business owners to not move ahead with their business until they have investigated every last detail of the business they want to start and are absolutely sure it's all going to work and be profitable. The problem with that approach is that it leads to procrastination. No one ever really has all the pieces in place – even after they've started their business. Yes, you need to research the market, have a rudimentary plan in place and do things like get a tax id if needed, register with local officials, if required, etc. But if you try to make everything perfect before you launch, you may never get around to starting the business at all.

Keeping an eye on your competition should be an ongoing exercise. You should always be looking for that little something extra to set you apart from the crowd. It might be lower prices or deluxe service. However, you do it you need to distinguish yourself from others offering the same goods and services.


**Set your Corporation**

Many business owners today established corporations. Corporations are separate legal entities that you can use to operate a business. Corporations give you the advantage of limited liability meaning that you only risk the amount you invest in the company provided that you properly operate the corporation.

# CHAPTER 2

## Do You Need Excellent Credit to Start a Business?

The answer to this question is NO. you don't need good credit to start a business, but yes you will need good credit score to obtain funding for loans and business financing. Don't let this common problem deter you from stating your business. If you are startup business and have a poor (or nonexistent) credit history, here are a few tips that should help:

**1. Forget big banks as sources of funding.** In the past, obtaining bank financing was based on the four Cs of credit: credit history, cash flows, collateral and character. Today, this is no longer true for most large, well-known financial institutions. They care little about three of the four Cs-and instead tend to focus purely on credit history in making lending decisions to small-business applicants. This is because consolidation in the banking industry has driven banks to automate their credit decision processes and minimize the labor involved in getting to know credit applicants face to face. If you have a great business idea but poor credit history (such as a credit score below 650), you will not get any money from banks. Even if you have a great business idea, a strong character and relevant work experience, you are not likely to get any money from big banks if your credit score is not above the 600 to 650 range.

**2. Differentiate your personal credit from your business credit.** While large banks focus on your personal credit score, smaller community lenders and business-friendly banks will focus on a combination of your personal credit score, business credit score and other factors associated with the viability of your business.

Your personal credit score is determined by several factors, including the outstanding debt balance on personal credit cards, the number of open lines of credit accounts, bill payment history and late payment history. Your business credit score is determined by similar factors but is linked to the tax ID for your business, not your Social Security number. This important difference can help you get your business off the ground.

If your personal credit score is damaged, you should seriously consider getting a separate tax ID number for your business as soon as possible-whether you are incorporated or not. If you do not want to spend the money to incorporate your business, you can still get a tax ID number from the IRS even if your business is a sole proprietorship, an LLC or a partnership. Talk to your CPA for information on how to do this. It's very simple to complete the relevant form (form SS-4) and send it to the IRS. You can apply online at the IRS site.

**3. Build your business's credit score.** Once you have a tax ID number and a legal identity for your business, you can start building your business's credit and establishing a means to qualify for trade and credit lines from suppliers and sources of capital.

A growing number of data companies currently track business credit. For example, Equifax has recently developed the Small Business Financial Exchange which provides participating banks with a business credit report. This report contains information on your business's performance on open lines of credit, including credit cards, installment loans and even loans between relatives, friends and business associates that are reported to Equifax. If you are able to keep these loans on track by making your payments on time, you can establish a strong credit rating for your business.

There are several other data companies that collect financial information on your business. D&B's PAYDEX score is among the most famous. This score allows your suppliers to know the likelihood that you will be delinquent on a payment. Specifically, the score measures the extent to which payments to your existing vendors have been made on time over the past 12 months. However, keep in mind that most small vendors do not report to D&B. To maximize the likelihood that your business's PAYDEX score is high (more than 70 out of 100), you should focus on paying large vendors who are likely to submit information to D&B.

If you do not have strong personal credit, you should pay special attention to ensuring that you build a good business credit history with companies like Equifax and D&B.

# CHAPTER 3

## Start Your Business in One Day

**Get over the company-name thing.**

Many people agonize endlessly over dreaming up the perfect company name. Don't. If you're waiting until you come up with the perfect name, you're also waiting to start making money.

Instead, at least for now, forget branding and unique selling propositions and all the business-identity stuff. And don't worry about finding the perfect URL or website design or promotional literature. You're putting those carts way before your business horse, too.

Just pick a name so you can get the administrative ball rolling.

Remember, your business can operate under a different name than your company name. (A "doing business as" form takes minutes to complete.) And you can change your company name later, if you like.

## 2. Get your Employer Identification number (EIN).

An EIN is the federal tax number used to identify your business.

You don't need an EIN unless you will have employees or plan to form a partnership, LLC, or corporation. But even if you don't need an EIN, get one anyway: It's free, takes minutes, and you can keep your Social Security number private and reduce the chance of identity theft, because if you don't have an EIN, your SSN identifies your business for tax purposes.

Note: If you're using an online legal service to set up an LLC or corporation, don't use it to get your EIN. Instead, apply online at the IRS website. You'll have your EIN in minutes. Www.irs.gov

## 3. Apply for a Duns & Bradstreet Number.

This is for your business credit dunsbradstreet.com

## 4. Register your trade name.

If you won't operate under your own name, your locality may require you to register a trade name. In most cases, you'll get approved on the spot.

**5. Business Phone line** (Phone Number) Google Voice, Magicjack.com, VOIP numbers or personal cell phone

**6. Get your business license.** Your county or city will require a business license. The form takes minutes to fill out.

Use your EIN instead of your Social Security number to identify your business (for privacy reasons if nothing else).

**7. Complete a business personal-property tax form** (if necessary). Businesses are taxed on "personal" property, just like individuals. Where I live, no form is required for the year the business is established.

If you are required to file a business personal-property tax form and you plan to work from home using computers, tools, etc., that you already own, you won't need to list those items.

If you purchase tangible personal property during your first year in business, you will list those items when you file your business personal-property tax form the following year.

**8 Ask your locality about other permits.**

Every locality has different requirements. In my area, for example, a "home occupation permit" is required to verify that a business based in a home meets zoning requirement.

Your locality may require other permits. Ask. They'll tell you.

**9. Get a certificate of resale (if necessary) State Local Tax Commission**

A certificate of resale, also known as a seller's permit, allows you to collect state sales tax on products sold. (There is no sales tax on services.)

If you will sell products, you need a seller's permit. Your state department of taxation's website has complete details, forms, etc., if you decide to apply online, but most localities have forms you can complete while you're at their administrative offices.

**10. Get a business bank account.**

One of the easiest ways to screw up your business accounting and possibly run afoul of the IRS is to commingle personal and business funds (and transactions). Using a business account for all business transactions eliminates that possibility.

Get a business account using your business name and EIN, and only use that account for all business-related deposits, withdrawals, and transactions.

Pick a bank or credit union that is convenient. Check out your local credit unions; often they provide better deals than banks.

# CHAPTER 4

## Choosing Your legal Setup

You have decided to start a business. You now must determine your legal structure. Visiting your states local website. Most can be done online for a low cost and do not have to be filed through a lawyer or third party. Doing your research will save you a lot of money in the long run.

Apply for Federal Tax ID (This is your social security for your business.) You can apply for this online for free from the www.IRS.gov website. This is what most banks and lenders will ask you for upon applying for business accounts and lines of credit.

You also need to apply for Duns & Bradstreet which is building business credit as well. You can apply online from www.DNB.com. This is also another free step.

Google voice number offered by Google and magicjack.com online services are fast easy and affordable sources for business phone lines. You don't have to spend hundreds of dollars on a separate line to make more bills for your business keep cost simple and low to start.

# Friendship & Partnership

### 1. Friendship Does Not Translate into Business Compatibility

When starting a business venture with a friend or beloved family member, it is tempting to believe that your existing relationship will easily translate into a successful commercial union.

This is rarely the case, however, as even people with similar values and philosophies may not share the same approach to completing various business tasks. This can create significant 2. Friends and Family Rarely Plan for Worst Case Scenarios

### 3. It Can be Difficult to Create Clearly Defined Business roles

The majority of friendships are formed organically, which means that there are no predetermined roles or structural hierarchies. The same cannot be said for business partnerships, which are forged by choice and constructed to include individual roles and responsibilities. This almost always requires one partner to take an authoritative, leading role, which can create imbalance in an existing friendship and ultimately cause unrest.

There may be a tendency among friends and family members to avoid this entirely, but this may expose the business to a critical lack of leadership.

## 4. Your Business Goals May Differ from Those of Your Partner

On a similar note, your motivation for launching a business may differ to that of your friend or family member. For example, while you may aim to realize the long-term goal of launching a successful business, your partner may want nothing more than to earn some additional money to supplement their existing income. This is entirely opposed to the foundation of commercial partnerships, which should be formed from a common goal and fixed business aspirations.

Such a gap in expectations can be devastating, as it can trigger arguments, undermine business growth and compromise friendships.

**5. The Price of Failure is Far Higher**

According to industry statistics and successful entrepreneur Such failure often comes at a considerable cost to small-business owners, although this is often restricted to financial losses.

conflict when establishing a business model or cultivating a company culture, which in turn has the potential to undermine even the most durable of relationships.

# What You Should Know When Choosing Among the Types of Business Entities

Your choice of business entity is a very important one. It can affect how people perceive your business and has a big impact on your legal exposure and finances.

Keep the following in mind when deciding among the different types of business entities:

Sole props and general partnerships are good "starter" entities.

As your business grows and generates more income, consider registering as an LLC or corp.

Think through the pros and cons of each business entity in terms of legal protection, tax treatment, and government requirements. Consult a business lawyer and accountant to get specific help for your business.

## Setting Up Sole Proprietorship

Sole proprietorship is easier to set up than corporations or other entities. To establish a sole proprietorship, you typically need to file fictitious name certificate at a local or stage government office. If you're doing business under a name different than your own. This certificate in essence notifies the world who the business's true owner is, such as, "Paul Smith, DBA Red Wings Flowers." The DBA abbreviation stands for "doing business as."

**\*Key points characterize sole proprietorship**
**Business transferability -**
**Existence** – after you die or become disabled, business may have difficulties continuing
**Expenses** – must keep records of your personal expenses

**Licenses** – you may need carious business licenses, sale licenses or permits

Tax – the IRS taxes you and your business as one from for income tax purposes

## Creating a Partnership

You can set up your business as a partnership consisting of two or more partners. Partnerships come in three types (general, limited, and limited liability.)

General Partnerships consist of two or more partners. General partnerships tend to be easy to establish and can be more informal than business entities like corporations.

Limited Partnerships consist of one or more general partners and one or more limited partners. The general partners typically get to make all business decisions and the limited partners are typically passive investors. A limited partnership requires you to file an organizational form certificate with the secretary of state.

Limited Liability Partnerships are new entity authorized by certain state laws LLP's are basically general

partnerships with liability shield for partners. LLP's are typically taxed as pass through entities with partners not the entity paying taxes on the business's name.

**C Corporations** have limited liability are well understood entities that can accommodate many businesses. On the downside corporations require that you follow a fair number of formalities and make several governmental fillings.

**S Corporations** are corporations that can meet certain requirements and that affirmatively elect to be taxed as a S corporation.

## Sole Proprietorship Pros and Cons

A sole proprietorship is the simplest business entity, with one person as the sole owner and operator of the business. If you launch a new business and are the only owner, you are automatically a sole proprietorship under the law. There's no need to register a sole proprietorship with the state, though you might need local business permits or licenses depending on your industry.

Freelancers, consultants, and other service professionals commonly work as sole proprietors, but it's also a viable option for more established businesses, such as retail stores, with one person at the helm.

### Pros of Sole Proprietorship

Easy to start up (no need to register your business with the state).

No corporate formalities or paperwork requirements, such as meeting minutes, bylaws, etc.

You can deduct most business losses on your personal tax return.

Tax filing is easy—simply fill out and attach Schedule C-Profit or Loss from Business to your personal income tax return.

## Cons of Sole Proprietorship

As the only owner, you're personally liable for all of the business's debts and liabilities—someone who wins a lawsuit against your business can take your personal assets (your car, personal bank accounts, even your home in some situations).

There's no real separation between you and the business, so it's more difficult to get a business loan and raise money (lenders and investors prefer LLCs or corps).

It's harder to build business credit without a registered business entity.

Sole proprietorships are by far the most popular type of business structure in the U.S. because of how easy they are to set up. There's a lot of overlap between your personal and business finances, which makes it easy to launch and file taxes. The problem is that this same lack of separation can also land you in legal trouble. If a customer, employee, or other third party successfully sues your business, they can take your personal assets. Due to this risk, most sole proprietors eventually convert their business to an LLC or corporation.

## General Partnership (GP) Pros and Cons

Partnerships share a lot of similarities with sole proprietorships—the key difference is that the business has two or more owners. There are two kinds of partnerships: general partnerships (GPs) and limited partnerships (LPs). In a general partnership, all partners actively manage the business and share in the profits and losses.

Like a sole proprietorship, a general partnership is the default mode of ownership for multiple-owned businesses—there's no need to register a general partnership with the state.

## Pros of General Partnership

Easy to start up (no need to register your business with the state). No corporate formalities or paperwork requirements, such as meeting minutes, bylaws, etc.

You don't need to absorb all the business losses on your own because the partners divide the profits and losses.

Owners can deduct most business losses on their personal tax returns.

## Cons of General Partnership

Each owner is personally liable for the business's debts and other liabilities.

In some states, each partner may be personally liable for another partner's negligent actions or behavior (this is called joint and several liability).

Disputes among partners can unravel the business (though drafting a solid partnership agreement can help you avoid this).

It's more difficult to get a business loan, land a big client, and build business credit without a registered business entity.

Most people form partnerships to lower the risk of starting a business. Instead of going all in on your own, having multiple people sharing the struggles and successes can be very helpful, especially in the early years.

That being said, if you do go this route, it's very important to choose the right partner or partners. Disputes can seriously limit a business's growth, and many state laws hold each partner fully responsible for the actions of the others. For example, if one partner enters into a contract and then violates one of the terms, the party on the other side can personally sue any or all of the partners.

## Limited Partnership (LP) Pros and Cons

Unlike a general partnership, a limited partnership is a registered business entity. To form an LP, you must file paperwork with the state. In an LP, there are two kinds of partners: those who own, operate, and assume liability for the business (general partners), and those who act only as investors (limited partners, sometimes called "silent partners").

Limited partners don't have control over business operations and have fewer liabilities. They typically act as investors in the business and also pay fewer taxes because they have a more tangential role in the company.

## Pros of Limited Partnership

An LP is a good option for raising money because investors can serve as limited partners without personal liability.

General partners get the money they need to operate but maintain authority over business operations.

Limited partners can leave anytime without dissolving the business partnership.

## Cons of Limited Partnership

General partners are personally responsible for the business's debts and liabilities.

More expensive to create than a general partnership and requires a state filing.

A limited partner may also face personal liability if they inadvertently take too active a role in the business.

Multi-owner businesses that want to raise money from investors often do well as LPs because investors can avoid liability.

You might come across, yet another business entity structure called a limited liability partnership (LLP). In an LLP, none of the partners have personal liability for the business, but most states only allow law firms, accounting firms, doctor's offices, and other professional service firms to organize as LLPs. These types of businesses can organize as an LLP to avoid each partner from having liability for the other's actions. For example, if one doctor in a medical practice commits malpractice, having an LLP lets the other doctors avoid liability.

## C-Corporation Pros and Cons

A C-corporation is an independent legal entity that exists separately from the company's owners. Shareholders (the owners), a board of directors, and officers have control over the corporation, though one person in a C-corp can fulfill all of these roles, so it's possible to create a corporation with you in charge of everything.

With this type of business entity, there are many more regulations and tax laws that the company must comply with. Methods for incorporating, fees, and required forms vary by state.

## Pros of C-corporation

Owners (shareholders) don't have personal liability for the business's debts and liabilities.
C-corporations are eligible for more tax deductions than any other type of business.
C-corporation owners pay lower self-employment taxes.

You have the ability to offer stock options, which can help you raise money in the future.

## Cons of C-corporation

More expensive to create than sole proprietorships and partnerships (filing fees range from $100 to $500 based on which state you're in).

C-corporations face double taxation: The company pays taxes on the corporate tax return, and then shareholders pay taxes on dividends on their personal tax returns.

Owners cannot deduct business losses on their personal tax return.

There are a lot of formalities that corporations have to meet, such as holding board meetings and shareholder meetings, keeping meeting minutes, and creating bylaws.

Most small businesses pass over C-corps when deciding how to structure their business, but they can be a good choice as your business grows and you find yourself needing more legal protections. The biggest benefit of a C-corp is limited liability. If someone sues the business, they are limited to taking business assets to cover the judgment—they can't come after your home, car, or other personal assets.

Corporations are a mixed bag from a tax perspective—there are more tax deductions and fewer self-employment taxes, but there's the possibility of double taxation if you plan to offer dividends. Owners who invest profits back into the business as opposed to taking dividends are more likely to benefit under a corporate structure. Corporation formation and maintenance can be complicated.

## S-Corporation Pros and Cons

An S-corporation preserves the limited liability that comes with a C-corporation but is a pass-through entity for tax purposes. This means that, similar to a sole prop or partnership, an S-corps' profits and losses pass through to the owners' personal tax returns. There's no corporate-level taxation for an S-corp.

## Pros of S-corporation

Owners (shareholders) don't have personal liability for the business's debts and liabilities.
No corporate taxation and no double taxation: An S-corp is a pass-through entity, so the government taxes it much like a sole proprietorship or partnership.

## Cons of S-corporation

Like C-corporations, S-corporations are more expensive to create than both sole proprietorships and partnerships (requires registration with the state).

There are more limits on issuing stock in S-corps vs. C-corps.

You still need to comply with corporate formalities, like creating bylaws and holding board and shareholder meetings.

In order to organize as an S-corporation or convert your business to an S-corporation, you have to file IRS form 2553. S-corporations can be a good choice for businesses that want a corporate structure but like the tax flexibility of a sole proprietorship or partnership

## Limited Liability Company (LLC)

A limited liability company takes positive features from each of the other business entity types. Like corporations, LLCs offer limited liability protections. But they have few paperwork and ongoing requirements, and in that sense, they are more like sole proprietorships and partnerships.

Another big benefit is that you can choose how you want the IRS to tax your LLC. You can elect to have the IRS treat you as a corporation or as a pass-through entity on your taxes.

## Pros of LLC

Owners don't have personal liability for the business's debts or liabilities.

You can choose whether you want your LLC to be taxed as a partnership or as a corporation.

Not as many corporate formalities compared to an S-corp or C-corp.

### Cons of LLC

It's more expensive to create an LLC than a sole proprietorship or partnership (requires registration with the state).

LLCs are popular among small business owners, including freelancers, because they combine the best of many worlds: the ease of a sole proprietorship or partnership with the legal protections of a corporation.

As a starting point, though, there are three general factors to consider when choosing among business entity types: legal protection, tax treatment, and paperwork requirements. In the table below, see how the entities

| TYPE OF ENTITY | LIMITED LIABILITY PROTECTIONS? | TAX TREATMENT | LEVEL OF GOV'T REQUIREMENTS |
|---|---|---|---|
| Sole proprietorship | No | Taxed at personal tax rate | Low |
| General partnership | No | Taxed at personal tax rate | Low |
| Limited partnership | For limited partners only | General partners taxed at personal tax rate | Medium |
| S-corporation | Yes | Taxed at personal tax rate | High |
| C-corporation | Yes | Must pay corporate taxes (but beware of double taxation on dividends) | High |
| Limited liability company | Yes | Can choose how you want to be taxed | Medium |

# CHAPTER 5

# Tax ID Number

**Tax Identification Number (TIN)** is a nine-digit number used as a tracking number by the U.S. Internal Revenue Service (IRS) and is required information on all tax returns filed with the IRS. Employer tax ID numbers are issued to businesses by the IRS. These numbers are also nine digits long, but they are read as XX-XXXXXXX.

The IRS uses tax identification numbers to track taxpayers. The IRS issues all tax identification numbers except for SSNs. Filers must include the number on tax-related documents and when claiming benefits.

The tax identification number is also known as the taxpayer identification number.

## EMPLOYER IDENTIFICATION NUMBERS

The IRS uses the Employee Identification Number (EIN) to identify corporations, trusts, and estates that must pay taxes. These groups must apply for the number and use it to report their income for taxation purposes. Applying for an EIN is free, and a business can obtain one immediately.

## INDIVIDUAL TAX IDENTIFICATION NUMBER

The IRS issues ITINs to certain nonresident aliens who do not otherwise qualify for an SSN. The spouse of a nonresident alien must include the number on his tax returns when he files. In order to get an ITIN, the applicant must complete Form W-7 and submit documents supporting his status as a nonresident alien. Certain agencies — including colleges, banks and accounting firms — are able to help applicants obtain their ITIN.

## Who needs an employer identification number?

The IRS uses your EIN to identify your business for tax administration purposes.

**Your small business can use an EIN to do any of the following:**

- *Pay federal taxes*
- *Pay your employees*
- *Open a business checking account*
- *Apply for business licenses and permits*

**ESTABLISH BUSINESS CREDIT WITH MERCHANTS AND VENDORS**

# Small Business Licenses and Permits:

## Local Small Business Licenses You Need to Know

Now, you might not need to obtain these small business licenses in the end, but it's worth going through this checklist just to make sure you don't need them. That way, you can be confident that you have everything you might need to legally run your business—and you won't be blindsided by a missing mandatory small business license down the line.

*These basic small business licenses might be required by your local, county, or city governments, so be ready to check for them all at the appropriate government office.*

## 1. Local Business Operating License

A basic small business license essentially grants you the right to operate your business.

You might need your local or city government to issue you a local small business license to operate within your town's or city's limits.

Your city's business license department will, of course, be specific to your location, so you need to locate the office on your own to obtain this small business license. If you don't know where to start, your best bet is to go to your local city hall or courthouse to find the office where can obtain your business license.

And if you're starting a business that technically is outside of your closest city limits, this general business operating license might come from your county's government office.

## 2. Zoning and Land Use Permits

Once you fill out and file your local business license application, the city zoning department usually checks to make sure that your business's location and area are zoned for your type of business and the parking area around your business meet the local zoning codes.

You might be starting a business in an area that's already been zoned for the type of business you're starting. *Lucky you*—no need to worry about adding specific zoning and land use permits to the list of small business licenses you need to obtain.

But you can't operate your business in an area if it's not zoned for your type of business. You need to get a variance or conditional-use permit in order to operate in that area. You'll need to present your case for business before your city's planning committee to get the variance. When you present your business for land use permits, you'll just need to show that operating your business in that area won't significantly disrupt the character and safety of the neighborhood you plan to operate in.

## 3. Building Permits

If you're lucky enough to be starting your business in the perfect space, maybe you won't need to worry about small business licenses and permits for your building.

But if you're planning on building an entirely new building, renovating an existing one, or installing new utilities or appliances in an existing one, you likely need to obtain building permits from your local government. This ensures that what you're building, or renovating is in line with safety codes and conforms to local requirements.

Your licensed contractor that you're working with should know everything you need to secure with your local government for your business.

## 4. Fire Department Permit

Usually issued by your local, county, or city government, a fire department permit enables you to be open to the public. A permit from your fire department is especially necessary if your business uses flammable materials.

Some cities require that you have these small business licenses from the fire department before you open your doors for business. Others just require periodic inspections and certificates of inspection to keep your business open.

Every business owner should check to see if they need a fire department permit. But businesses that serve the public—think restaurants, retirement homes, hotels, day-care centers, gym studios, etc.—definitely need these small business licenses.

## 5. Health Licenses and Permits

If you're operating a restaurant, starting a cafe, or opening a fitness facility—anything that could possibly relate to people's health, really—you should pay attention to these small business licenses and permits.

Most local governments have health permits that small businesses in the area need to operate. The requirements you face for your business, again, will entirely depend on your local government. So, go to your local town hall to figure out the health permits you need to operate your business in the area.

## 6. Signage Licenses and Permits

You might not have known it, but some cities and counties have restrictions on what your business's signage can look like. We're talking size, location, visibility, lighting, and so on.

If your business's signage isn't up to your local government's requirements—and you have the licensing and permits to show it—your business could suffer from some serious fines. So, to make sure your signs are legal, check in with your local government on what kind of small business licenses you need to follow signage codes.

## 7. Environmental Licenses and Permits

Environmental small business licenses and permits mostly fall at the state and federal government level, but it's worth mentioning while we're listing off your local small business licenses requirements.

Local governments are increasingly looking to protect their population and land's health by regulating small businesses in the area. Environmental permits might regulate where you can produce and sell, air and water quality levels in your area, and waste removal requirements. Air quality boards are popping up all over the United States, so it's important to check if you need a specific environmental license or permit with your local government.

## SMALL BUSINESS LICENSES FOR HOME-BASED BUSINESSES

Our small business licenses checklist has so far covered the documents that small businesses operating in commercial spaces need to know.

But what if like many small businesses out there, you operate your business out of your home?

If you run your business out of your home as a sole proprietor or consultant, you might not know that you too have a list of small business licenses and permits you need to secure. A lot of home-based business owners don't know this and are fined for it.

*So, what do you need? Here are the basic small business licenses you should gather before operating your home-based business:*

### 1. Home Occupation Permit

Almost all home-based small businesses need a Home Occupation Permit to legally operate. Consultants or freelancers might *only* need a Home Occupation Permit as a small business license.

A *Home Occupation Permit* essentially just shows that by operating your business out of your home, you aren't significantly adding traffic, noise, or harmful environmental conditions to your area.

### 2. Property Use and Zoning Permits

Small business owners operating out of their homes should be aware of local zoning ordinances that apply to home-based businesses in their area.

Residential areas can have *strict zoning regulations* that might even prevent home-based businesses altogether. Don't worry—it could be possible to get a variance that lets you operate out of your home. Again, check with your local or city government office to know what the rules and regulations are regarding home-based businesses in your area.

## 3. General Business Licenses and Permits

Most home-based businesses have to go through the *same* process to get the small business licenses that *any* business needs to operate.

*If you're a home-based business owner, you still likely need to have the following:*

General business license

Professional and trade licenses for certain industries

Sales tax permits

Health, safety, and environmental permits

Signage permits

Building and construction permits

Unfortunately, you can't dodge these general small business licenses as a home-based business owner. You, along with all other small businesses, will need to have these on your files in order to operate your small business legally.

## Small Business Licenses and Permits

## : The Next Steps

Once you've dutifully made your way through your small business licenses checklist and secured all the documents you need on hand to operate, what's next?

Well, now you can focus your attention on the important stuff—launching and growing a successful small business.

As for small business licenses, most of the heavy lifting is done. But you still need to be aware of managing and maintaining your small business licenses and permits—you want to make sure you're *always* operating legally

So, you now have all tracked down and applied for the small business licenses and permits you need, display them properly, make copies for your own records, and keep track of your licenses and permits renewal dates.

Don't let these documents get dusty and lost in your file cabinet— keep a close eye on them, always updating when the time comes around!

# CHAPTER 6

## Build Business Credit

Some business entities, such as sole proprietors or self-employed individuals, may not be required to have an EIN. But some choose to get one anyway, to help protect themselves against identity theft or to identify as an independent contractor while working for pay.

For the purposes of building business credit, having an EIN is important because business credit-reporting bureaus can use it to report your business activities and payments.

An employer identification number, or EIN, is a tax identification number assigned by the IRS to small businesses, corporations and other types of business entities for tax purposes. Choosing your legal setup

You have decided to start a business. You now must determine your legal structure. Visiting your states local website. Most can be done online for a low cost and do not have to be filed through a lawyer or third party. Doing your research will save you a lot of money in the long run.

Apply for Federal Tax ID (This is your social security for your business.) You can apply for this online for free from the www.IRS.gov website. This is what most banks and lenders will ask you for upon applying for business accounts and lines of credit.

You also need to apply for Duns & Bradstreet which is building business credit as well. You can apply online from www.DNB.com. This is also another free step. Your business will need to have a main phone number to be listed with your business which can be found online or other searchable places such as Google, Bing, Yelp and other business directories. Being easily accessible is a major step in building your business credit. You want your customers and vendors to be able to find you easily when trying to determine if they should extend you credit.

Google voice number offered by Google and Magicjack.com or other great VoIP online services that are fast easy and affordable sources for business phone lines. You don't have to spend hundreds of dollars on a separate hard line and make more bills for your business. Keep cost simple and low to start.

Now that you have chosen your business name and got your basic information set up business phone number you must have a business entity.

## Duns & Bradstreet

Dun & Bradstreet (D&B) provides a D-U-N-S Number, a unique nine-digit identification number, for each physical location of your business. D-U-N-S Number assignment is FREE for all businesses required to register with the US Federal government for contracts or grants.

Business entities may request the DUNS number by calling a toll-free telephone number: 1-(866) 705-5711. Tell the operator that you are applying to a Federal financial assistance program and need to register for a DUNS number.

## How long does it take to get a DUNS number?

The standard process for acquiring a DUNS number is to go to the D&B website, figure out how to navigate their site, fill out 10 pages of complicated, unnecessary information about your company, and then choose to wait 30 days for a free DUNS number or pay $50 to get it in 5 days

Dun & Bradstreet is a corporation that offers information on commercial credit as well as reports on businesses. Most notably, Dun & Bradstreet is recognizable for its Data Universal Numbering System (DUNS numbers); these generate business information reports for more than 100 million companies around the globe.

**Can I use my DUNS number to apply for credit?**

D&B keeps track of businesses around the world by giving each a nine-digit DUNS number. This number is mainly used when businesses seek credit from other businesses. ... If you have a sole proprietorship, you can just use your SSN (and not an EIN) on a business credit card application.

## How to Build Business Credit for a Small Business

Establishing business credit is an important step for any new small business and helps you to: (1) maintain a credit history separate from your personal credit history and experience the business benefits of having good business credit, and (2) demonstrate separation between owners and the business.

## Why separate credit histories?

By having a business credit history separate from your personal one, you can minimize the effect negative events on one might have on the other. For example, if you have some financial missteps that impact your personal credit history and score, they shouldn't impact your small business credit if you have established a clear separation and vice versa.

## Why separate business and owners?

Unless you're operating your small business as a sole proprietorship or general partnership, you need to demonstrate that the business is separate from the owners. One of the key benefits that corporations and limited liability companies (LLCs) provide the owners is protection of their personal assets. Keep this protection in place by consistently showing clear separation between the owners and the business.

## Eight Steps to Establishing your Business Credit

1. Incorporate your business. Even though you may be incorporated when you're reading this, it deserves a mention. With sole proprietorships and general partnerships, the business is legally the same as the owner; therefore, there can be no separation of business credit history from personal. Incorporating a business or forming an LLC creates a business that is legally separate from the owner(s).

2. Obtain a federal tax identification number (EIN). The EIN is basically a social security number for a business. It is required on federal tax filings and is also required to open a business bank account in the name of the

corporation or LLC. In order to comply with IRS requirements, many larger businesses also require an EIN from their vendors in order to pay them for services provided.

3. Open a business bank account. Open a business checking account in the legal business name. Once open, be sure to pay the financial transactions of the business from that account. If you use a business credit card (see below) for many financial transactions, be sure to pay the credit card bill from your business checking account.

4. Establish a business phone number. Whether you use a landline, cell phone or you use VoIP, have a separate number for your business and in your business's legal name. List that number in the directory so it can be found.

5. Open a business credit file. Open a business credit file with all three business reporting agencies: Experian, Equifax and TransUnion.

6. Obtain business credit card(s). Obtain at least one business credit card that is not linked to you or any other owners personally. Pick a business credit card from a company that reports to the credit reporting agencies.

7. Establish a line of credit with vendors or suppliers. Work with at least five vendors and/or suppliers to create credit for your company to use when purchasing with them. Ask them to report your payment history to the credit reporting agencies.

8. Pay your bills on time. Perhaps it should go unsaid but be sure to pay your bills on time. Like with your personal credit, late payments will negatively impact your business credit.

# CHAPTER 7

## What's Your Business Plan

Every business starts with an idea. Regardless of what the idea is, a well-thought-out business plan is what helps transform an idea into a reality. It is a common misconception to think that business plans are written for the sole purpose of obtaining financing. Actually, the most important reason for writing a business plan is to create an essential management tool to use in the present, as well as the future.

## Write Your business plan

Now that you have your idea in place, you need to ask yourself a few important questions: What is the purpose of your business? Who are you selling to? What are your end goals?

How will you finance your startup costs? These questions can be answered in a well-written business plan.

A lot of mistakes are made by new businesses rushing into things without pondering these aspects of the business. You need to find your target customer base. Who is going to buy your product or service? If you can't find evidence that there's a demand for your idea, then what would be the point?

Conducting thorough market research on your field and demographics of potential clientele is an important part of crafting a business plan. This involves conducting surveys, holding focus groups and researching SEO and public data.

A business plan helps you figure out where your company is going, how it will overcome any potential difficulties and what you need to sustain it. A full guide to writing your plan can be found here, and when you're ready to put pen to paper, these free templates can help.

## Getting Your Business Plan Setup

A written document fully describing and analyzing a particular business; it provides complete, detailed information about short- and long-term business plans. Information providing potential investors with complete knowledge of a business; investors will then be able to understand all of its strengths and weaknesses, enabling them to identify present and future potential

# Getting Started Today and Not Tomorrow!

What do you need to do to start a business? There are plenty of sites and books that tell you all the things you should do. Although such checklists are very useful because they help you remember important start up steps, they are just To Do lists. They tell you what to do, but don't provide any tips about what makes a business successful.

Unfortunately, you don't succeed in business just by completing a list of tasks. Nor will your business be a success just because you think it's a good idea.

## DETERMINE YOUR LEGAL BUSINESS STRUCTURE

Before you can register your company, you need to decide what kind of entity it is. Your business structure legally affects everything from how you file your taxes to your personal liability if something goes wrong.

If you own the business entirely by yourself and plan to be responsible for all debts and obligations, you can register for a sole proprietorship. Be warned that this route can directly affect your personal credit. Alternatively, a partnership, as its name implies, means that two or more people are held personally liable as business owners. You don't have to go it alone if you can find a business partner with complimentary skills to your own.

If you want to separate your personal liability from your company's liability, you may want to consider forming one of several types of corporations. This makes a business a separate entity apart from its owners, and therefore, corporations can own property, assume liability, pay taxes, enter into contracts, sue and be sued like any other individual. One of the most common structures for small businesses, however, is the limited liability corporation (LLC). This hybrid structure has the legal protections of a corporation while allowing for the tax benefits of a partnership.

*Ultimately, it is up to you to determine which type of entity is best for your current needs and future business goals.*

More details about the different business structures can be found here.

1.    **Know yourself, your true motivational level**, the amount of money you can risk, and what you're willing to do to be successful. Sure, we all want to make millions of dollars. But what are you willing to give up reaching that goal? How many

hours a week will you work on an ongoing basis? How far out of your comfort zone are you willing to stretch?

How far will your family stretch with you? To be successful, keep your business plans in line with your personal and family goals and resources.

2.      **Choose the right business for you.** The old formula – find a need and fill it – still works. It will always work. The key to success is finding needs that you can fill, that you want to fill, and that will produce enough income to build a profitable business.

3.      **Be sure there really is a market for what you want to sell**. One of the biggest mistake's startups make is to assume a lot of people will want to buy a particular product or service, because the business owner likes the ideas or knows one or two people who want the product or service. To minimize your risk for loss, never assume there is a market. Research the idea. Talk to real potential prospects (who aren't family and friends) to find out if what you want to sell is something they'd be interested in buying, and if so, what they'd pay for the product or service.

4.      **Plan to succeed.** If you're not seeking investors or putting a huge sum of money into your business, you may not

need an elaborate business plan, but you still do need a plan - one that specifies your goal – your destination – and then lays out at least a skeletal road map for how you'll get to where you want to go. The plan will change as you progress and learn more about your customers and competition, but it will still help you stay focused and headed in the right directions. Use our business planning worksheet to help develop that basic plan.

**Don't procrastinate.** I've heard some people advise would-be business owners to not move ahead with their business until they have investigated every last detail of the business they want to start and are absolutely sure it's all going to work and be profitable. The problem with that approach is that it leads to procrastination. No one ever really has all the pieces in place – even after they've started their business. Yes, you need to research the market, have a rudimentary plan in place and do things like get a tax id if needed, register with local officials, if required, etc. But if you try to make everything perfect before you launch, you may never get around to starting the business at all.

## GETTING YOUR BUSINESS PLAN SETUP

A **written document** fully describing and analyzing a particular business; it provides complete, detailed information about short- and long-term business plans. Information providing potential investors with complete knowledge of a business; investors will then be able to understand all of its strengths and weaknesses, enabling them to identify present and future potential

# Why Create a Business Plan?

**A COMPLETE BUSINESS PLAN WILL:**

Assist management in obtaining various sources of financing

Identify the strengths and weaknesses of a business

Present correct details about the business; i.e. past, present, and future performance

Furnish detailed projections about the company

Discuss the financial aspects of starting or expanding the business

Guide management through the steps of developing and fine-tuning a business

Provide clear business objectives and short- and long-term goals

Provide answers for any potential financial backers

Provide prospective investors with the information to determine whether the company is the correct investment for them

Provide a chronology of events and financial markers against which the firm can compare their actual results

Keep a business focused

Improve odds for success

Chances of receiving funding are dependent on the accuracy and completeness of the business plan

## THINGS TO CONSIDER WHEN DEVELOPING A BUSINESS PLAN:

Four basic questions to guide you in developing the business plan:

**What are the firm's own success strengths and weaknesses?**

**What is the overall business concept?** Manufacturing, retail, or service sector?

**What is the current situation?** Develop an overview of the business operation, focusing on the competitive environment What is the current financial picture?

**Products and/or Services:** What the business offers to the customer in the marketplace

**Operations Analysis:** How the company's infrastructure is going to work

**Marketing and sales operations:** How the business is going to create the need for the product/service

**Developing the financials of a business plan:** Projects how the business will perform in the future

**Cover letter:** States why the business owner is creating and submitting the business plan

**Highlight important information from the plan.** If the business plan is being presented to a specific individual, make certain his/her name and address is spelled correctly

**Non-disclosure statement:** This informs the reader to keep the plan's contents confidential

**Title page:** Contains the following information:

-Current date   -Company logo   -Company name   - Company address   -Company email address

-Company telephone numbers   -Home and office #s of employees   -Company Web site address

**Table of contents:** Should specifically outline core sections and sub-sections of the business plan; it is a good idea to wait until the plan is written before adding page numbers

**Executive summary:** This section is the most important part of any business plan and should be written when the plan is complete; **if you can't sell the plan in the executive summary, your plan has less chance of being read;** it should include:

**Business Description:** Must specifically state what the business is and why it will be successful.

Vision statement describes where you want to be. Mission statement describes how you will get there; it is what makes a business unique

**What are the opportunities for the business?** Discuss the market and the industry. What are the competitions?

**What is the marketing/sales strategies?** What are the financial?

What is the profit potential like? What are the sales projections?

What is the growth potential? What personnel are needed?

What is the product/service?

## What Is My Business?

## *If the company is:*

**A MANUFACTURING BUSINESS:**

-What is the source of the competition?

-Is there available skilled labor to hire?

-Will the products be made for inventory or per order and how much of each are made?

## A RETAIL BUSINESS:

-By what means will the business be kept current of fashion changes and taste changes in the business?

-How will the advertising needs be handled?

-How much actual inventory should be purchased?

-Should the store open in a mall or a free-standing location?

## A SERVICE BUSINESS:

-Are the **skills** better than competitors?

-Should the business insist on **cash payments** only?

-Identify he **market**(s) to be served -Should **franchising** be considered?
-Identify the business' competitive **advantage**

-Is the **client list** big enough or should the business start fresh?

-Explain how the business' product/service is **different** from competitors

-Explain the **legal structure** of the company; is it a sole proprietor, partnership of corporation? Be as specific as possible

-Tell the reader if the business is a **start-up** or identify the length of time it has been in business

-Provide a brief **overview** of progress to date; be sure to mention contracts, patents and any market research identifying the viability of the business

-Describe the **management team**, as well as their individual experience

-Indicate exactly how much money has been invested and how it has been spent

-Summarize the past **financial performance** by identifying the projected gross revenues and net profits -Explain if management will be drawing a **salary** from the business in the beginning, if so, be as specific as possible when quoting the salary requirements

**What Does Legal Structure Mean?**

**What is the legal structure of the business (if selling equity)?**

**GENERAL PARTNERSHIP:** A business partnership featuring two or more partners where each partner is liable for any debts taken on by the business

-All the partners' **assets** can be involved in a bankruptcy case against the company

-Both groups are usually **involved** in day-to-day operations

**LIMITED PARTNERSHIP:** A business organization with one or more general partners who manage the business and assume legal debts and obligations, as well as one or more limited partners, who do not participate in day-to-day operations and are liable only to the extent of their investments

**CORPORATION:**

-The most common form of business organization; chartered by a state and given many legal rights as an entity separate from its owners

-Characterized by the limited liability of its owners and the issuance of shares of easily transferable stock

# CHAPTER 8

## Business Banking 101

When Opening a business bank account, you want to arrive early and dress the part of a successful business person, just as if you were going on your first interview for a new job. You want to present your business and yourself with your new banker or bank. A first impersonation is a lasting impersonation. You want to have your original copies of your legal business documents readily available in a folder or envelopes. Depending on your legal suture will determine if you your credit or banking history will affect the opening of your business account.  Some banks will require the sign officers to have a high credit or good banking back ground. Opening a business bank account makes it easier to keep your business and personal cash flow separate.

If you're searching for a good small business checking account, consider Bank of America. It has low fees - waived in some cases - and one of the largest branches and ATM networks nationwide. This makes Bank of America the best checking account for most small business owners.

### 1. CHOOSE THE BEST TYPE OF BUSINESS BANK ACCOUNT

Most new business owners start by opening a business checking account. They must decide between a free online checking account, which is fine for most businesses without the need for cash deposits, or bank accounts with traditional banks which often come with more fees but also a wider variety of products and services. New business owners may also want to open a business savings account to earn interest on capital that's not ready to be deployed.

## Free Business Bank Account

Free business bank accounts are typically online providers that either don't charge monthly maintenance fees or make it easy to avoid them by meeting certain criteria, such as minimum balance requirements. They offer features such as electronic deposits, withdrawals, electronic transfers, and the ability to write checks.

They're best used for business with no cash deposit needs and brand-new businesses.

## HOW TO OPEN A BUSINESS BANKING ACCOUNT IN 5 STEPS

Opening a business bank account is a five-step process that includes determining the right type of bank account, selecting the right bank, knowing what you have to pay, providing the required documentation, and depositing funds. Opening a business bank account makes it easier to keep your business and personal cash flow separate.

If you're searching for a good small business checking account, consider Bank of America.

 It has low fees - waived in some cases - and one of the largest branches and ATM networks nationwide.

This makes Bank of America Chase Bank, Wells Fargo and Local Credit Unions the best checking account for most small business owners.

## THERE ARE 5 STEPS NEEDED WHEN OPENING A BUSINESS BANK ACCOUNT

Business owners should have both a business savings account and business checking account to separate their working capital and savings funds. However, it's important to be careful with CD accounts because you're required to leave your funds in the account for an extended period of time.

## Gather the Required Account Opening Documentation

When opening a business account, you'll typically need to provide documentation that verifies the name and general nature of your business.

You'll also need to show documentation that proves your business is registered with the IRS and indicates that you have the legal authority to set up the account. The exact documentation you'll need to provide will vary based on corporate structure.

## Sole Proprietorship Business Bank Account Requirements

You're a sole proprietorship if you're the sole owner of a business and have not filed paperwork to be another entity type like a limited liability company (LLC) or corporation.

**With sole proprietorships,** there is no legal distinction between you — the owner — and your business. This means that you are not only entitled to all the profits but also all the potential losses or debts. The key proprietorship business bank account requirements for documentation are:

**Personal identification:** You'll need your Social Security number as well as two forms of personal ID to open a business bank account; valid types of identification include a driver's license, passport, and Social Security card

**Fictitious business name certificate:** You might also need a "Fictitious Business Name" certificate known as a "doing business as" certificate (DBA certificate) if your business operates under a different name from your own

## LIMITED LIABILITY COMPANY BUSINESS BANK ACCOUNT REQUIREMENTS

Your business is a limited liability company (LLC) if you've filed articles of organization with the state. You can fall out of good standing if you fail to file paperwork or pay fees to the state on time, which needs to be corrected before you can open a bank account.

You'll also typically be required to have an LLC operating agreement. Unlike a sole proprietorship, an LLC is a separate entity from the owners, and the owners are protected from some personal liability for business debts and obligations.

When you form an LLC, you can choose to organize your company either as an S-corp or a partnership. That said, the LLC business bank account documentation requirements will be similar to those required for the entity structure you choose.

## The key LLC business bank account requirements for documentation are:

• Business identification:

To open a business bank account, you'll need your federal EIN as well as a copy of your articles of organization •

**Organizational documents:**

You'll need to provide the organizational documents used to form either your S-corp or partnership

• Other potential documentation:

• You also may need to provide a signed declaration of unincorporated business and any required business licenses; business licenses are common with healthcare businesses or restaurants

## C CORPORATION BUSINESS BANK ACCOUNT REQUIREMENTS

You're a C corporation if you have filed articles of incorporation with the state. Similar to S-corps and LLCs, you can fall out of good standing if you don't pay the state or fail to file paperwork. As with a partnership, LLC, and S-corp, a C-corp is an entity separate from the business owners. With a C corp, the company is liable for the company's debts and obligations. The owners, or shareholders, are not personally responsible.

The key C-Corp business bank account requirements for documentation are:

• **Business identification:** Like an LLC, you'll need your federal EIN to apply for a business bank account

- **Articles of incorporation:** Additionally, you'll also need your certified articles of incorporation; you'll receive your article of incorporation documents as a part of your incorporation process
- **Corporate charter:** If your articles of incorporation don't provide sufficient information regarding who is authorized to sign, you may also need to provide an additional corporate charter that specifies this information
- **Corporate resolution:** You might also need to provide a signed corporate resolution by all of your officers as well as a signed signature card by the account signers
- **Business licenses**: Businesses that need a license will need to provide their license documentation like health care businesses or restaurants

## BENEFITS OF OPENING A BUSINESS BANK ACCOUNT

The primary benefit of opening a business bank account is that it's an excellent way to separate your business and personal finances. Additionally, if you have excess funds that you want to keep liquid but also want to earn interest on, a savings account can be a great solution. Lastly, a business bank account is one of the first steps to set yourself up for a simplified tax season. Some of the primary benefits of a business bank account are:

•        Separate your business & personal finances: Having your business and personal bank accounts separate can help increase your business credit score; if you have an unexpected financial event in your personal life, it won't affect your business credit score

•        Maintain a clean financial record: A business bank account can help provide a clean financial record at the end of the year because your personal finances won't be commingled with your business; some bank accounts even integrate with the leading accounting software, which can simplify your income tax season

•

The IRS also requires businesses to maintain records of their transactions, such as income and expenses. A business bank account makes it much easier for business owners to provide these records to the IRS."

Opening a business bank account can serve as a key beneficial step for any new business. You can separate your finances to make for an easy tax season and earn interest on your savings for future projects. There are things you should do to keep in mind while you're in the process of opening your first business bank account.

## What Do I Need to Open a Business Bank Account?

Business bank account requirements vary depending upon how your business is structured like a sole proprietorship, LLC or Corporation.

In general, you'll need to provide proof of your personal or business identity like a driver's license or EIN, the documents used to organize your business like an operating agreement and copies of any business licenses.

### Which Bank Provides the Best Free Business Checking Accounts?

When searching for the best free business checking account, you should consider fee structures and transaction limits.

# CHAPTER 9

# Choosing Your Location

Your new location is an exciting part of the small business adventure. Choosing your business location, you want to make sure zoning, parking, competition in your area. Adjacent business doesn't just concentrate on price.

**MANUFACTURING**

-Where will the business be located?

-Where is the majority of the customer base located? This will affect shipping costs - Where are the suppliers located?

**SERVICE**

-Where will the business be located?

-Where is the distance from the customer base?

-What foot traffic does the location have?

-What are the demographics of the area?

**RETAIL**

-What will the hours of operation be?

-Where will the store(s) be located?

-What foot traffic does the location have?

-How easy is it to get into the store?

-What are the demographics of the area?

## Leases for Your Business (Rent)

You need to do a cost analysis between buildings to properly estimate your business's future rental costs.

Any analysis of a given space's desirability typically begins with the fixed rent that the landlord quotes you. But you have to evaluate this starting point in light of other factors.

For example, landlords may quote a monthly lease rate of $2 per square foot, typically meaning rent able square footage. The actual usable square footage of the premises is the space that you actually can use for your business operations. The structure of the lease payments may also be important. For example, a start-up business without much capital may want two or three months of free rent at the beginning of the lease, with a lower rental for the first year and increasing rentals for the second and third years.

When analyzing the cost of space, you must also take into account other operating costs that the landlord may pass on to you, the tenant. Some leases require the tenant to pay for all cleaning, building security, air-conditioning, maintenance, and so on (a so-called Triple Net Lease). And some leases require the landlord to provide and pay for basic services, while the tenant pays a proportionate share of any cost increases that the landlord incurs for such services over the initial base year of the lease. Keep in mind that different buildings have different costs, and landlords may charge for services in a different manner. So, the types and amounts of the costs that the landlord passes on to the tenant can have a big impact on the economics of a lease.

## NEGOTIATING PERMITTED USES

The lease typically has a section that sets forth the permitted uses of the leased space.

Making this permitted use clause as broad as possible works to your advantage as the tenant, even if you initially have a narrow-intended purpose.

Because your business may grow and your plans may change, you want the flexibility to use the space in any reasonable, legal manner.

Also, a narrow-permitted use clause can often serve as a restriction on your ability to assign or sublet the space.

So, what's the best permitted use clause? See if you can get the landlord to agree to something like the following:

Tenant is permitted to use the premises for any legal purpose or business.

If the landlord doesn't go for that, at least spell out all of your expected or potential uses.

## Working out the term of lease

Fixed rent over longer term leases is relatively rare, because landlords often try to build in rent escalation provisions.

Sometimes, landlords insist on annual increases based upon the percentage increases in the Consumer Price Index (CPI). If you're confronted with such a request, do two things to make rent increases manageable:
Try to arrange that the CPI doesn't kick in for at least 2 years.

Try to get a cap on the amount of each year's increase (for example, no more than a 3 percent increase in any year).

## Operating costs

The starting point for determining your operating costs is identifying what services the landlord provides, what services the tenant must get directly, and who bears the cost. The following are typical costs for office space:

Heating, ventilating, and air conditioning (commonly referred to as HVAC)

Cleaning and janitorial services

Electricity

Repairs

Security

If the landlord is charging you separately for such services, try to negotiate a fixed fee or cap on the amount.

Looking into security deposits

**WHAT PROCESS?**

How will your business do? Master your process of sales, collecting money, orders, making and receiving phone calls getting new business. Practice the process

How will the product/service be made/performed?

## STAGE OF DEVELOPMENT:

-What are the problems in the development of the product/service?

-Indicate which industry associations the owners of the business will affiliate with -Are there any industry guidelines that must be complied with?

-Are there any government regulations that management must follow?

-Who are the suppliers to the business?

-Are there alternate suppliers for backup?

-What are their prices, terms and conditions?

## PRODUCTION PROCESS:

-What are basic requirements for the business? Consider land, equipment and office space. Management should be familiar with these costs

-When will production begins on the product or service?

-How long will it take to produce the products?

-Be familiar with the costs of all materials

-Who will make purchases on the components necessary for production?

-How will the company respond if the demand for goods fluctuates?

-Did the company perform feasibility testing on their product (testing of the process, prototyping and pricing)?

-What will be the system for keeping track of inventory?

# CHAPTER 10

## 10 Tips to Help You Build A Successful Small Business Brand

### 1. Be unique. What makes your business unique?

What's your story? What do you do that others in your industry do not do?

### 2. Grow your community.

Many of the world's best brands, including Google, Amazon, Facebook, Virgin, and Skype, spend modest sums on advertising and instead, focus on building and improving their communities. Those companies understand that if people trust a brand's community, they will extend trust to the brand.

Small businesses have many opportunities to build online and offline communities. For example, you can build online communities on Twitter, Facebook, your small business blog, on Instagram, or on other social networks. And remember that you can't be in all places at once. Pick one or two places where you can focus building your community and invest your time and resources there.

## 3. Build great products and services.

Consider that the number one reason people write about brands is to share experiences

## 4. Have a good name and logo.

A strong brand is easily recognizable. Recognition starts with the name of your business. The name will appear on your business cards, letterhead, website, social networks, promotional materials, products, and pretty much everywhere in print and online to identify your company or your company's products and/or services.

## 5. Find your voice.

What you say is important, but don't overlook how you say it. Your company's "voice" is the language and personality you and your employees will use to deliver your branding message and reach your customers. Successful brands speak with a unique voice. Think about the brands you admire – what makes them unique? How do they communicate with you and other customers? What do you like about their voice?

**6. Be consistent.** Many small businesses mistakenly change their messaging depending on their audience. For example, a company might take a more serious tone on their website but a very lighthearted tone on their Facebook fan page. This can confuse your customers and potential customers. To build and maintain a strong brand, every aspect of your brand should be as good as your product or service and you must be consistent in presenting your brand. This includes not only your company's name, logo, overall aesthetic design, products and services, but also includes your marketing materials, website, appearances at trade shows and conferences, content posted to social networks, etc.

Why should you care about brand consistency?

You should care because brand consistency leads to familiarity, and familiarity leads to trust.

## 7. Keep your promises.

Although this is common sense, you'd be surprised how many small businesses tarnish relationships with their customers by failing to keep their promises. Happy customers who feel good about your business are your best source of referrals.

## 8. Stand for something.

Think about brands you love. Those brands commonly stand for something (or against something) and connect with their customers emotionally. One of my favorite companies, 37signals, develops software to help people collaborate. 37signals believes that most software is bloated and difficult to use. They don't compete on features – they compete on usability. They have developed a reputation as a company that stands for easy to use software.

What does your business stand for (or against)?

## 9. Empower your customers.

You are not in control of your brand. You can set your brand's direction, but how your brand is perceived is determined by your customers and potential customers. People can become your brand's ambassadors – spreading your ideas and brand to their own networks. Spend time nurturing relationships with such people. Who are they? What can they give and get in order to help your brand? Ultimately, successful brands recognize that if they help their customers succeed, the customers will in turn help the brand succeed.

**10. Deliver value.** Value doesn't always mean lowest price. You can focus on product leadership (having the best products in the marketplace, like Apple), operational excellence (having the lower prices in the marketplace, like Ikea), or great customer service (Virgin, Zappos). You can also focus on a combination of those things.

As you think about the value your company delivers – you can ask the following questions: What sets your product, service and company apart from your competitors? What value do you provide and how does that value differ from that provided by your competitors? Think about which of the benefits are emotional – the most powerful brands tap into emotions.

## KNOW YOUR MARKET AND CUSTOMERS

Conduct a market analysis: Market research that supplies information about the marketplace This involves:

**Competitive Analysis:**

One must know who the competition is and what they are doing; competition is the rivalry among firms operating in a market to fill the same customer need

-

**Competitive intelligence**

is the publicly available information on competitors, current and potential; it has 3 parts:

**-Defensive intelligence:**

Information gathered to avoid being caught off guard; serves to keep track of moves that deal with the firm's business

**-Passive intelligence:**

information obtained for a specific decision (i.e. a company may seek information about a competitor's return policy when developing its own)

-

**Offensive intelligence:**

Identifies new opportunities

-Awareness of all current and potential business opportunities and risks in the marketplace

-An extensive understanding of the nature of the competition both direct and indirect to help obtain competitive advantage; complete a review of the industry, as well as the primary competitors -Familiarity with the strengths and weakness of the competition

## Customer Analysis:

Businesses compete to serve consumer needs

-Define the consumer needs

-What are their buying patterns?

**-What is the market potential: What is the total demand for a product in an environment?**

Measured by:

-Market size

-Market growth

-Profitability

-Type of business decisions and customer market potential

-Define the customer's purchasing decisions

-What is the make-up of customers and the target market?

Include demographics like age, gender and income

# CHAPTER 11

## Marketing Plan

*Describe the marketing strategies one will use to influence the customer to purchase the product or service*

### MARKETING MIX:

The "four Ps" of marketing, price, product, place, and promotion

**Price:** The four factors used to arrive at a price:

**Pricing objectives**

**Cost**

**Competition**

**Demand; ask and answer the following questions:**

-Is the product or service better than those of its competitors?

-If the price is lower, how will the business be able to charge less?

How will the price of products/service compete with market prices?

If price is higher, why would a customer choose the product?

-Is the company offering discounts to students, seniors or for those who pay in cash rather than by credit?

Does the company sell in large volume?

How are similar products/services priced?

-

Is the quality different and/or is the production process more efficient?

-Provide a brief summary of the fixed and variable costs. What do the costs include?

-

What kind of a return is management looking for in the investment and how soon does the business anticipate recouping the investment?

**Pricing Strategy:** Determine the price of the product and/or service

**Skimming pricing:** Setting a high price during the initial stage of the product's life

**Penetrating pricing:** Setting a low price during the initial stages of the product's life; promote heavily at this time to gain market share
Established products

**Maintaining the price:** Pricing that maintains position in the marketplace and builds on the product's public image

**Reducing the price:** Cut price to meet or beat that of competition

**Increasing the price:** To segment the current served market and to take advantage of product differences Price-Flexibility Strategy:

**One-price strategy:** Charging the same price to all customers based on same conditions and quantities; helps to simplify pricing decisions and to keep goodwill among customers

**Flexible-pricing strategy:** Charging different prices to different customers for the same product and quantity; price is based on customer value (financial worth) to the business

## PRODUCT/SERVICE STRATEGIES

**Product/services strategies** state market needs that may be served by different product offerings What are the business' products and/or services?

Evaluate all of the firm's products and/or services

Understand the consumer perception of a product and/or service compared to the competition

Identify the one thing that makes the product or service unique

What other features does the product/service have? Consider quality, price, convenience, selection, packaging and service

Identify benefits customers will experience from buying the product/service

**Product-Positioning Strategy:** Introducing a brand in the marketplace

Where will it be received favorably compared with competing brands?

This will help position the product so that it stands apart from the competition

**Product-Repositioning Strategy:** View the current status of the product and find a new position that seems like it will work better

Increases the life of the product

Corrects an original positioning mistake

**New-Product Strategy:** A new product introduced to meet new needs and to continue competitive pressure on existing products

**Value-Marketing Strategy:** Delivering on promises made for the product or service; promises of product quality, customer service, and meeting time commitments; geared toward total customer satisfaction

## SALES/DISTRIBUTION PLAN

Describe the type of person/business likely to buy the product/service

What is the distribution of the product or service? Will the company use mail-order, wholesaler, retailer? Describe the return policy Describe the service guarantees and any other warranties What post-sales support will be offered?

What payment plans will be offered? Identify
specific marketing materials to be used
Identify cost of advertising

How much business is anticipated from these
sources?
What are the costs for various services? Will the company use the Web?

## SALES/DISTRIBUTION STRATEGIES

**Channel-Structure Strategy:** The process of using intermediaries in the slow of goods from manufacturers to customers; distribution can be direct or indirect; reaches the largest number of customers as quickly as possible, at a low cost, but still maintaining control

**Multiple-Channel Strategy:** When there are two or more different channels for distribution of goods and services; achieves greatest access to each market segment to increase business

## PROMOTION:

Creates awareness, gets the buyer to buy and describes how a product/service solves the buyer's need What is the position you want to hold in the customer's mind?

Creating a consistent message when communicating the product's position; it is what the business wants the customer to think of when he/she sees their brand the following are some promotional tools:

**-Sales and sales management-Advertising:**

 Trade publications      -Trade shows      -Promotional materials

**Advertising: Direct mail**

        -Internet -Packaging -Public relations -Television -Radio

The main purpose of advertising is to build brand awareness and create a new want or awareness of the product; must identify ways of advertising the product/service

identify the cost for advertising Identify necessary marketing material specifically

## Promotion strategies

-**Media-Selection Strategy:** Choose channels (i.e. newspapers, magazines, television, etc.) through which messages for the product/service are transmitted to the customer; helps move the customer along the desired path of the purchase process

-**Advertising-Copy Strategy:** Designing the content of an advertisement to communicate a product/service message to the potential customer

-**Selling Strategy:** Moving the customer to the purchase phase of the decision-making process through personal contact

*Pay your taxes. Federal, state local licenses and permits no matter big or small.*

# 9 Directories Your Small Business Needs to Be Listed On

As an added bonus, listing your small business on these sites can have a positive effect on your place in search engine results. The end result is that customers have an easier time purchasing your products and services online.

### 1. GOOGLE MY BUSINESS

Google My Business is the local directory of the world's most popular search engine. Not only does listing your small business here help you get found by searchers, but it also ensures your brick-and-mortar location shops are listed correctly on Google Maps. All of this means that customers can find your store with greater ease. Google My Business also lets small businesses post photos, discount offers and answer clients' feedback.

### 2. BING PLACES FOR BUSINESS

Widely touted as one of the most popular search engines, Bing created Bing Places for Business as a way to help small businesses get found on Microsoft's search engine. Not only does Bing Places let companies add up to 10 categories so customers can find them more readily, but it also features map locations, photos and customer reviews from Yelp.

### 3. YAHOO LOCAL

Yahoo Local lets owners list their businesses for free, but charges extra for premium services and cross-listing across Yahoo's network. As an added bonus, the directory offers easy-to-use tools for tracking impressions and evaluating overall search performance.

### 4. YELP

It's no secret that many searchers turn to Yelp before trying a new places or scheduling contractors, so it's an important local directory on which to list your small business. Not only can companies collect and respond to customer feedback, but they can also post special offers and use the Yelp reporting tool to stay on top of trends.

### 5. FOURSQUARE

Fifty million people currently use Foursquare, which lets users share information about their favorite businesses online. Unlike some of the other online directories listed, foursquare lets users check in when they visit businesses and even comment on their experiences via their Twitter accounts. Additionally, businesses can use the mobile app to target and connect with customers on the go

### 6. MANTA

Designed with the needs of the small business owner in mind, Manta offers a variety of products including paid ads and a listing manager that lets owners supervise multiple directories from a single location. And with 20 million plus users searching for businesses, there's a good chance that your website will get some attention.

### 7. MERCHANT CIRCLE

Along with helping your company enhance its rankings on Google, Bing and Yahoo, **MerchantCircle** lets owners build out their business listings with coupons, photos, newsletters, event postings and even videos. Further, the Merchant Circle Lead Store provides owners with valuable tips on customers who are actively searching for products and services.

### 8. CITYSEARCH

If your business isn't listed on City search, you might be missing out on an opportunity to grow your customer base. A popular choice among restaurants and entertainment businesses like spas, City search goes beyond directory listings by regularly creating local guides to help customers find the best of the best in a given city.

9. ANGIE'S LIST

Angie's List is a great place for primarily service-based businesses to showcase their offerings. With more than 2 million users, businesses have a strong chance of being found. As an added benefit, reviews are never anonymous, and must be verified by BPA World wide's certification process.

# Chapter 12

## Why a Business Needs Money

First, let's take a look at why a business needs money in the first place. There's no uniform "startup" fee for building a business, so different businesses will have different needs. It's important to first estimate how much you need before you start finding alternative methods to fund your company.

**Consider the following uses:**

- Licenses and permits. Depending on your region, you may need special paperwork and registry to operate.

- Supplies. Are you buying raw materials? Do you need computers and/or other devices?

- Equipment. Do you need specialized machinery or software?

Office space. This is a huge expense, and you can't neglect things like Internet, utilities costs, janitorial services and whether to outsource back office tasks, like payroll and invoicing.

- Associations, subscriptions, memberships. What publications and affiliations will you subscribe to every month?

- Operating expenses. Dig into the nooks and crannies here, and don't forget about marketing.

- Legal fees. Are you consulting a lawyer throughout your business-development process?

Employees, freelancers and contractors. If you can't do it alone, you'll need people on your payroll.

## 1. REDUCE YOUR NEEDS

Your first option is to change your business model to demand fewer needs as listed above. For example, if you were planning on starting a company as a consultant or freelancer, you could reduce your "employee" expenses by being the sole employee at the start. Unless you need office space, you can work from home. You can even do your homework to find cheaper sources of supplies or cut out entire product lines that are too expensive to produce at the outset. There are a few expenses that you won't be able to avoid, however. Licensing and legal fees will set you back even if you cut back on everything else. According to the SBA, many micro-businesses get

## 2. BOOTSTRAP

Your second option invokes the idea of a "warmup" period for your business. Instead of going straight into full-fledged business mode, you'll start with just the basics. You might launch a blog and one niche service, reducing your scope, your audience and your profit, in order to get a head-start. If you can start as a self-employed individual, you'll avoid some of the biggest initial costs (and enjoy a simpler tax situation, too). A payment processing company, such as Due, can be a big help when you are struggling to invoice and follow up professionally.

Once you start realizing some revenue, you can invest in yourself, and build the business you imagined piece by piece, rather than all at once.

## 3. Outsource

Your third option is all about getting funding from outside sources. I've covered the world of startup funding in a number of different pieces, so I won't get into much detail, but know there are dozens of potential ways to raise capital -- even if you don't have much yourself. Here are just a few potential sources for you:

- Friends and family. Don't rule out the possibility of getting help from friends and family, even if you have to piece the capital together from multiple sources.

- Angel investors. Angel investors are wealthy individuals who back business ideas early in their generation. They typically invest in exchange for partial ownership of the company, which is a sacrifice worth considering.

- Venture capitalists. Venture capitalists are like angel investors but are typically partnerships or organizations and tend to scout businesses that are already in existence.

- Crowdfunding. It's popular for a reason: with a good idea and enough work, you can attract funding for anything.

- Government grants and loans. The Small Business Administration (and a number of state and local government agencies) exist solely to help small businesses grow. Many offer loans and grants to help you get started.

- Bank loans. You can always open a line of credit with the bank if your credit is in good standing.

## WHAT CAN YOU GET FOR FREE FOR YOUR **BUSINESS?**

Another successful key to be a successful Entrepreneur is cutting cost before you inquire the expense and also learning to be cost effective. Figuring out what you can get for free or discounted for your business from the start will save you money and time in the long run. You want to seek out the free adverting, legal aids, office spaces, business cards, inventory management and customer leads sources. I recommend sites such as www. Freesite.com and shop around on the internet for cost cutting techniques.

**FREE ADVERTISMENT**

Gaining coverage in local papers, trade magazines and websites can greatly increase name recognition and educate people about your business - driving new customer acquisition. While many growing businesses in competitive landscapes may want to hire an expensive public relations firm, startups and small businesses can start off with some simple "do-it-yourself" PR.

## INCREASE LEAD GENERATION AND CUSTOMER ENGAGEMENT WITH EMAIL MARKETING

Entrepreneurs don't need to pay an agency or marketing consultant to develop an email campaign either. You can do it yourself with free services, which allows small-business owners to send marketing emails, automated messages and targeted campaigns to customers. If you want to get more personal and send one-on-one messages, there are many sites that you can use that automatically notifies you when someone opens an email you sent them.

## LEVERAGE SOCIAL MEDIA

It's free, easy to get started and offers a massive network of potential customers. The hard part is increasing your followers without wasting your precious time. Make sure you focus on value over volume. Identify the social channels that reach your customers best – including Facebook, Twitter, Pinterest, Instagram, LinkedIn and the new guy, Ello.

The goal is to provide your followers with something that's useful, interesting and shareable. Start small, post a few times a week and learn who your audience is. Once you have an understanding of who's consuming your content, and what they're interested in, you can start ramping up efforts.

Satisfied clients can be a business's best marketing tool. Actively engage pre-existing clients through PR, social media and email.

For example, pitching your business and a satisfied customer to a writer can be mutually beneficial for both parties. This tactic generally leads to a more compelling story and a stronger relationship between you and your customer. Once you have a customer army of spokespeople, let them share positive experiences and tell your company story for you.

Marketing a small or new business is extremely crucial to a company's success but that doesn't necessarily mean you have to invest a huge chunk of capital into it. Savvy, frugal entrepreneurs can find products and services that can help increase visibility and drive customer acquisition – without spending any overhead.

### DON'T MIX BUSINESS AND PERSONAL EXPENSES

There are so many reasons not to mix your business and personal accounts, including tax issues, personal liability, and jumbled accounting records, just to name a few. When things get tight, resist the urge to secure your business finances with personal funds because it will surely create a mess you will have to deal with later on.

The best way to maintain clear separation of your expenses is to set a personal budget and a business budget. Adhere to them strictly and separately so that credit cards and loans for your business don't get used for your personal finances and vice versa. Your bookkeeper and **accountant** will thank you for not muddying the money waters when it comes time to manage your books and pay your taxes.

### 2. NEGOTIATE WITH VENDORS BEFORE SIGNING A CONTRACT.

Sometimes you have to dig a little for a good bargain. When making purchases from vendors or contracting with suppliers, try negotiating for a better deal. Don't forget to examine purchase terms like late payment penalties and grace periods when making a decision. Sometimes being given an extra 30 days to pay can save you more than a 5% discount off the top.

### 3. PAY YOUR BILLS ON TIME, EVERY TIME.

Just as you do with your personal finances, it's important that you pay all of your business bills diligently. Credit card and loan payment late fees can cost you dearly but paying small late fees on vendor and utility bills consistently adds up, too. The same goes for taxes: paying too late can result in serious penalties.

Set up monthly reminders to make sure there are no business bills falling through the cracks. For young businesses especially, the profit-loss margins are thin. Avoiding late fees could be the difference between ending the year in the red or in the black.

### 4. MAKE FRUGALITY A HABIT.

You don't have to turn yourself into an extreme couponed to save money on ordinary business expenses. Follow through on mail-in rebate offers for office equipment and supplies, buy furniture and major equipment secondhand, and go green to save money on utilities.

## 5. SPEND SOME TIME IN AN INTRODUCTORY ACCOUNTING CLASS.

Being a small business owner doesn't automatically make you a whiz with money, but you'll still have to make big money-related decisions for your company. So even if you hire a bookkeeper or work with an accountant, you should know the basics of business accounting. Take an Introduction to Accounting course online or at your community college if you need to and learn how cash moves in and out of your small business.

The more you understand your business finances and cash flow, the better prepared you'll be to make smart money management decisions. And, while these tips will get you started, nothing replaces being proactive and hands-on when it comes to managing your money—no matter how big or small the financial challenge.

Accounting in your small business doesn't just involve keeping the books for tax purposes, but it is an important device for saving money and identifying waste, fraud, and theft. That's why It's so important for business owners to hire professional accountants instead of trying to do the books themselves or delegating the work to inexperienced staff members. Even successful companies can easily go broke because of accounting mistakes that result in unpaid taxes, fraud, theft or embezzlement.

## Most Common Accounting Mistakes

Accounting mistakes include making basic math errors, entering data incorrectly and failing to document expenses and income. The following accounting mistakes are among the most common for small businesses.

## Organization

In accounting, organization is critical. That means keeping receipts for all expenditures, using business credit or debit cards for expenses, keeping the books up-to-date, noting petty cash expenses accurately on the day that they're incurred and not mixing personal and business finances.

As a busy business owner, it is easy to pick up supplies while doing your personal shopping and errands. However, it is important to get separate receipts and use your state resale ID number for any supplies that will be resold. Although expenses under $75 don't generally require a receipt, it's always a good idea to get one. When you can show receipts for all your expenses, auditors are less likely to challenge them.

## GETTING BEHIND ON PAPERWORK

Small business owners tasked with wearing many hats frequently put off doing the books until the end of the week or the end of the month--or later. This is a risky strategy because it's easy to get behind on financial statements, reports that must be filed, sales tax payments, bill payments and even billing customers for money that they owe you.

Delayed billing can result in bounced checks, increased debts that will never get paid and mistakes in invoices that will be difficult to prove at a later date. You could be liable for penalties and interest for filing reports late or lose out on big financial opportunities because the books aren't current. If you have to struggle or rush to catch up on your books, it's easier to make costly mistakes.

## MATH ERRORS

The IRS often discovers math errors and corrects them for you. However, you can't count on any agency catching your math errors. There are also other kinds of math errors that agencies can't identify, and these can have a significant cumulative effect on your finances. These kinds of errors include entering figures in the wrong place, failing to round off figures properly or making errors that are not in your favor.

## HIRING THE WRONG OFFICE STAFF

If the person in charge of doing your books doesn't know what he or she is doing, you're the one who pays for any errors. No employee, relative or casual acquaintance will worry about your books as much as you or a professional accounting company will. If such a person makes a mistake, he or she isn't invested like an accountant with a fiduciary responsibility or a person with a financial interest in the business. The other risk of hiring someone who is not a professional is that the person could easily engage in criminal activity like embezzlement or theft.

## BEING UNWILLING TO DELEGATE

Small business owners are often unwilling to delegate bookkeeping to **experienced accounting professionals**, yet business growth depends upon the critical ability to let other professionals handle anything outside of your business core competencies.

Simply, you must be willing to let other people do their jobs while you do yours. Few business owners are qualified in accounting, tax strategies, managing business assets and setting up business entities to capitalize on the advantages of certain business structures. You need expert advice and an experienced accountant to maximize income and minimize taxes.

## POOR COMMUNICATIONS

Poor communications between you and your **bookkeeper** can result in serious mistakes in your records, filing reports, and result in everything from impossible to reconcile statements to inaccurate key financial data. It's easy to forget that you paid someone a bonus in cash or gave a cash discount unless you write the information down and convey it to your bookkeeper.

Technology doesn't prevent accounting mistakes because of the "garbage in, garbage out" business adage. The person who enters the accounting numbers in software and technology applications needs to transfer them correctly and enter them in the right place at the right time. The bookkeeper needs to know when to file paperwork and how to interpret facts about assets, taxes and other matters.

If you want to get the most profits from your sales and expenses, you need to utilize an experienced accountant or **bookkeeping service** to handle your books the right way to help you avoid errors, find savings on taxes and uncover other business opportunities based on your financial picture. At the very least, ensure proper procedures and processes are in place to keep communication open and productive.

## GETTING PAID (4 DIFFERENT PAYMENT METHOLDS)

### CASH

"Cash is king" as they say, but is this the best option for your customer base? Many businesses choose to be a "cash only" business for various reasons. Some businesses choose to operate on a "cash only" basis so that they can (illegally) report less on tax documents. Be aware, however, that this can make you a bigger target for tax audits. Other businesses do so because they can't afford the merchant fees that come with processing credit and debit card payments. Accepting cash at your small business should always be the starting point, but you should not stop there

## CHECKS

Accepting checks seems to be an outdated and risky way of accepting payment, but many businesses still do so. It's difficult for small businesses to verify whether checks are good or if the account has insufficient funds. Having a check "bounce" will not only hurt your business's bottom line, but can incur additional fees depending on your financial institution's policy

## Credit Cards

Credit card payment is the leading method of payment in the world next to cash. This method, however, often comes at a cost. Many credit card companies charge transactional fees (assessed per transaction), flat fees (assessed per month), and incidental fees (assessed under certain situations such as charge-backs). Visa and Mastercard dominate the market as they are widely accepted worldwide. American Express and Discover are the next big players but have a lower acceptance rate given their higher processing fees.

# CHAPTER 13

## UNDERSTANDING YOUR FINANCIALS

How financially viable will the business be? Why is it necessary to determine amount and type of all expenses? It is imperative to show expected results for the first and/or current year of operation. Up to five years of future projections are necessary. A business plan for an on-going business should include financial statements from the previous five years. Financial projections should be realistic. This section will serve as a benchmark for the company to gauge progress against original projections. Determine amount and type of all expenses the business will incur; this basic information will help create the financial statements for the business; these statements are:

Balance sheet: A "snapshot" of the financial state of the business at a particular point in time.

-It outlines the assets, liabilities and equity -It helps one understand the net worth of the business

-Balance sheet should list current assets, such as Accounts Receivable, Cash Balances and Inventory

-It should also list fixed assets, such as property, equipment, furniture and fixtures, and vehicles

-**Current liabilities** include accounts payable and debts that must be paid within a year; normally, these debts are payable to creditors and suppliers

-Long-terms liabilities include long-term loans made to the business

-**Shareholder's equity** consists of permanent funds contributed to the business by owner; also, shareholder's equity can be contributed by someone who invests in the business for a share of ownership (capital stock) and retained earnings

Income Statement

    -Shows the profit or loss for a particular time period

    -Details all revenues, expenses and other costs; as with the cash-flow statement, it should be prepared monthly, or quarterly

    -It is an accounting tool used to measure business performance

    -Reveals the break-even point for the business (the point at which the level of sales in either dollars or units causes revenue to equal total costs)

    Statement of Cash Flows

-A reflection of how much money the business has at a particular point in time

-If the cash inflows (collected revenue) exceed the cash outflows (disbursements), the cash flow is positive

-If the cash outflows (disbursements) exceed the cash inflows (collected revenue), the cash flow is negative -A cash-flow statement enables one to see exactly where cash is low and when the company will have a surplus; it should be prepared on a monthly basis

-The important point is anticipating and planning for fluctuations

-There is an essential difference between cash flow and income statement

-The cash-flow statement includes details of time when revenue is collected, or expenses are paid

**EXPENSES:** All businesses have two (2) types of expenses - one-time expenses and operating expense

One-time expenses are costs incurred only once when first setting up a business; one-time expense examples are:

Cars and trucks

Decorating, remodeling, installation of equipment, fixtures and leasehold improvements

Deposit or down payment on equipment (computers, photocopiers, etc.) and fixtures

Down payment on property or deposit on rent

Incorporation costs - where applicable

Licenses and permits

Product and development costs or franchise fees, where applicable

Promotion costs in anticipation of business opening

Starting inventory

Utility installation fees

**Operating expenses** are ongoing costs to be pad every month. Operating expense examples are:

-Distribution costs -Electricity fees-Insurance fees-Maintenance fees

-Promotion fees-Other financial expenses, i.e. sales discounts and bad debts

-Repayment of loan capital and interest-Auto expenses      -Travel expenses -Fees for accountants and lawyers

## ANALYSIS

**Benefit-cost analysis:** Used to compare advantages and disadvantages of various solutions to a specific problem the management team must first perform the following five (5) functions:

-Fully define the problem-Determine the objectives

-Develop alternatives -Attach a dollar value on all benefits and costs of each alternative

-Calculate the Benefit - Cost Ratio - (objectives divided by alternatives, B + C) and make the decision

**-Qualitative Models:** Reliance on expert judgments by professional managers

**Break-even analysis:** Use to determine at what point the company's costs match its sales volume (Fixed expenses + gross profit margin = sales to break even)

# Chapter 14

## Tax Deductions Checklist for Small Businesses

It is true that business owners get to enjoy some massive tax savings as compared to employees. However, more often than not, business owners do not take full advantage of all the tax deductions they are legally entitled to. Why? Because business owners often do not know WHAT deductions they can take!

It is never too late to get some tax saving strategies together. Since deducting expenses from your income reduces your tax bill, it's important to make sure you have captured everything you are legally entitled to! Use the following checklist as a guide to ensure you capture all your business expenses and minimize your tax bill!

### Checklist of Tax Deductions for Small Businesses

1. **Inventory (Cost of Goods Sold)**. Businesses that sell or manufacture products can deduct the cost of goods sold.

2. **Employees' Pay** You can deduct any amounts you give your employees f r compensation in cash, property or services.

3. **Employee Benefits.** Benefits like health plans, adoption assistance, educational assistance, and life insurance for your employees are generally tax deductible.

4. **Profit-Sharing or Pension Plans**. You can deduct contributions you make to your employees' SEP, SIMPLE, 401(k) and other qualified plans.

5. **Auto Maintenance and Mileage.** There are ways to calculate vehicle deductions

**: standard mileage rate or actual expenses (such as gas, repairs and maintenance). You may use the method that results in a larger deduction on your tax return.**

**Track your total auto expenses as well as business mileage so your tax advisor can help you to calculate the maximum deduction on your tax return!**

6. **Utilities. The water, power, trash, and telephone bills at your office are 100 percent deductible as regular business expenses**. If you have a phone number that has a mix of business and personal calls, you may still take a deduction for the portion relating to business usage.

7. *Home Office.* Rent, mortgage, insurance, electricity, housekeeping, security, maintenance, and many others are deductible items for your home office. Make sure to track costs incurred during the year and your tax advisor will help you to calculate the maximum benefit for the deduction!

8. *Travel Expenses.* Nearly all business travel expenses are 100 percent deductible. These include airfare, hotels, and other on-the-road expenses (like dry cleaning, Wi-Fi or cab fares). Eating out on the road is also deductible so don't forget to track these!

9. *Education. This includes seminars and trades how's*, don't forget any magazines, books, CDs and DVDs that are related to your business or industry. They are all 100 percent tax deductible. Also, travel to and from educational events are also tax deductions as well.

10. *Entertaining.* Eating out with colleagues on a day-to-day basis is *not* deductible, but if you bring along a client or prospective client, that meal is deductible. Taking a current or prospective client out for drinks or a show is also deductible, but it has to be within a business setting or take place before or after a business meeting.

**11.***Petty Cash and Tips.* Just because you didn't get a receipt doesn't mean you can't deduct the cost! Small cash expenses here and there can add up to a significant amount by the end of the year so make sure to track for these items!

**12.***Advertising and Marketing.* Be sure to deduct the cost of ordinary advertising (business card purchases, yellow page ads, website costs, Google ad words, and so on), as well as promotion costs for good publicity (such as sponsoring a local sports team).

**13.***Depreciation or Write-Off.* If you buy property to use in your business, you can take a tax benefit for it either in the current year or over time. Make sure to account for these purchases.

**14.** *Employee or Client Gifts.* A gift to a client or employee may be 100 percent deductible. **15.***Outside Help.* If you hire an independent contractor or family member, you can deduct their pay as a business expense.

**16.***Service Fees.* Those fees for processing credit cards? One hundred percent deductible.

**17.***Office Supplies.* Pens, paper, staples, thumb tacks... track these items because they DO add up!

**18.Bad Debts.** Your bad debt may be deductible if the amount owed to you was previously included in income. Make sure to speak to your tax advisor about this.

**19.Professional Fees.** Accountants, lawyers and other professional consulting fees are fully deductible.

**20.Furniture.** You can either deduct the entire cost in the year of the purchase or depreciate it over several years.

**21.Office Equipment.** That new fax machine, copier, or computer is also 100 percent deductible. You may be able to take it all in one year or depreciate it.

**22.Repairs and Maintenance.** The cost of repairs to keep your business property and equipment in operating condition is deductible.

**23.Insurance Premiums.** You can deduct premiums that you pay for credit, liability, malpractice, and workers' compensation insurance, among others.

**24.*Interest.*** Mortgage interest, finance charges (like credit cards), interest on payment plans, and interest paid on other loans are all 100 percent deductible.

**25.*Software.*** Boxed or downloaded software used for business are generally deductible. With more software being made available as a service, software subscriptions are also tax deductible.

**26.*Licenses.*** License, fees, permits, as well as regulatory fees, are generally deductible.

**27. *Taxes.*** As strange as it may seem, taxes incurred in running your business may be deductible!

## HOW TO PAY YOURSELF AS THE BUSINESS OWNER

You should only pay yourself out of your profits – not your revenue. When you see money coming into your business, don't assume you can pay yourself a big slice of that. Before you take your cut, you also need to take account of things like taxes, payroll, fixed costs and overheads. Setting your own salary will depend on your location, your industry, your profits, and how much you want to earn. But there are a few things to think about that can help you land on a reasonable figure.

## Don't undervalue yourself

If you're just starting a business, you might not turn a profit during your first year. Of course, this doesn't mean you shouldn't pay yourself.

Undervaluing your time and the work you're doing can harm your productivity and your business, so you should pay yourself enough to live comfortably without worrying. Take out what you need to avoid causing problems for your business and your personal life.

## Add yourself to the payroll and pay yourself regularly

Don't just dip into your business funds as and when you need to. Set up payments for you and your employees (it may be weekly or monthly) in your payroll software and stick to them.

Build that into your business plan right from the start, perhaps with a rising salary as your business grows. That way you'll get used to the amount of money you receive and won't have to worry about taking out occasional large lump sums.

## Take out 'reasonable compensation'

Depending on where you live in the world, 'reasonable compensation' or a similar term may apply to you. This is known as the amount of money that the government expects you to take from your business. It depends on the size of the business, the market sector and level of turnover and profit.

Here are some pointers for what's a 'reasonable' amount:

How much would a similar business pay for the work you do in your role?

What do recruitment ads and agencies offer to pay for someone in your position?

Are your wages equal to your duties and are those duties being performed?

Do your wages seem reasonable when you take into account of your level of responsibility and the amount of business you handle?

Is your pay directly related to the amount of time you spend working?

Does your pay seem reasonable when compared with your employees' wages?

## Consider the legal structure of your business

How much you can pay yourself, and when, might be restricted by the legal structure of the business you run.

For example, if you're a sole proprietor you're usually free to pay yourself whatever and whenever you like. That's partly because you're not accountable to shareholders or stockholders.

But other types of business, like incorporated businesses, usually have the business owner on the payroll. They would receive wages on a regular basis, just like any other employee.

## BE TAX EFFICIENT: FIVE POINTERS

Now you've decided how much is a fair salary for you, what's the best way to withdraw that money from your business while remaining as tax efficient as possible?

There's no one-size-fits-all approach because tax laws vary from one jurisdiction to another. Tax rates and allowances will also vary depending on how your business is legally structured. Here are some ideas to consider:

**Take a straight salary**
It's simple, easy to manage and account for, and is unlikely to raise any eyebrows. It's not always the most tax-efficient option, though.

**Balance salary with dividend payments**
If, as the business owner, you also own stock or shares in your company, you could take a minimal salary and then pay the remainder out of dividend payments. This can be more tax efficient (since dividends are usually taxed less than salary). Make sure you check the legality with your tax office first.

**Take payment in stock or stock options**
This can be a useful way of paying yourself in a tax-efficient manner.

**Take a combination of salary plus annual bonus**
This arrangement isn't just the preserve of the banking industry and it can be tax efficient in certain circumstances.

**Create a business agreement to pay yourself later**
If you're not desperate for money right now, you could create a written business agreement to pay yourself later, deferring payment to yourself. But this becomes a liability for the company and would need to be accounted for.

## Don't forget deductions, expenses and benefits

Leaving aside wages, there are some great financial benefits to running your own business. Medical insurance and 401(k) contributions are just two types of scheme to consider. They can make a big difference to your personal financial situation and they're legitimate business benefits.

Here are some examples of expenses that can be offset against the tax your company pays:

Car expenses (business mileage of your car)

Mortgage interest payments (if you work from your home)

Capital equipment expenditure (such as new computers).

You're not usually allowed to claim expenses in the "personal, living or family expense" category. But you can claim for the business use portion of an item. This might mean you get to drive a new car in your personal life at a reduced overall cost. When in doubt, check with your accountant to find out what will work for you.

Invest money for growth

Money you take out of the company (that doesn't relate to your business) is money that can't be used for investment and business growth. You're likely to be taxed on money you take out, so the real value of the money you keep in the company is even greater. That's because it will be untaxed or offset against tax, depending on how it's used.

If you think your business is going to grow in the future, it makes sense to use some of your profits to help that growth. The more money you invest sensibly into your business, the more likely it is that your company will grow. And that means you should be able to pay yourself more at a later date.

When not to pay yourself

If your business is going through a tough time financially, it's usually not a good idea to take any money out of your business for personal use.

You should avoid taking any money if your employees haven't been paid. It looks bad and would seriously affect their morale if you did.

When you owe a lot of money it's also wise to refrain from paying yourself a large amount. Creditors are unlikely to be impressed if you're still taking home a large pay packet while their invoices or loans remain unpaid.

Pay yourself what you deserve

Ultimately the amount you pay yourself will depend on the success of your business. The more money your business brings in, the higher the salary you could reasonably be expected to draw from it.

It makes sense not to get carried away and pay yourself too much, for reasons described. But if your company is profitable, there's no reason why you shouldn't reward yourself for that success.

"So early in my life I had learned that if you want something, you had better make some noise" -Malcolm X

# Chapter 15

## How to Run Your Business from Your Cell Phone?

Once looked upon as a measure of a business' reputation and size, utilizing cellular phones to conduct direct business with clients is no longer a practice that draws negative criticism. In fact, direct customer contact with cellular devices has increased to unprecedented levels in the past five years. It is no longer regarded as the shady business practice of fly-by-night companies but is now respected as a legitimate means to communicate with clients in an efficient and effective manner.

However, it is easy to get carried away and forget that a level of decorum is expected and sometimes forgotten with business cell phone usage. Running your business from a cellular phone does not have to be obvious. Many small business owners and entrepreneurs are choosing to take their cellular phones to the next level by adding Talk route to their service.

## Common Problems:

### MultiplePhones

So you are running your business from a cellular phone and it's wonderful! You can enjoy conducting business from the local park or attend your daughter's soccer game without missing any calls. You have shed the confines of your office and you are on your way to life without restrictions on your physical location. As the novelty of being able to go anywhere fades away, you realize that it is much more comfortable to use a desk phone in your home office and it is no fun to share your cell phone with that part-time employee you just hired. These minor annoyances begin to add up and you begin to wonder if running your business from a cellular phone was such a great idea.

### Your Cell Phone never closes

It's 5:30PM and you have just closed for the day, but your customers don't know it. Instead, you are receiving business related calls until the late evening hours. By not establishing times for when your cell phone is available to receive calls, you are telling your callers that you are a 24/7 business and those missed calls after hours are customers assuming that they are being ignored!

## Giving out your phone number

If there is one major disadvantage to running your business from your cellular phone, this has to be it. Nobody wants to give their cellular phone number out as a primary contact for their business.

# CHAPTER 16

# The Benefits of Being Mobile First

As a small business owner, you want to run a lean, profitable operation that makes running your business worthwhile. This chapter lays out a number of important benefits you can gain from a mobile first mindset.

## SAVING MONEY AND IMPROVING CASH FLOW

Saving money and to any small business. You simply can't succeed for very long if you aren't watching your bottom line. A mobile first approach offers real benefits that you can't afford to miss.

## Saving money

Buying the necessary equipment to run our small business can be expensive. Consider for example that if you decide you must have the latest iPhone, you're going to have an upfront expense of around $800. You'll likely encounter a similar capital outlay in another year or two when you want to replace it with the next big things. And that expenditure is only the beginning. you still need a service plan, apps and other addons to do the job properly.

Vendors like sprint can offer you a better option than simply putting out all that money up front. rather than buying, you may want to consider leasing equipment you need. With a lease you have low predictable monthly outlay on devices and services plan that can depend on. A lease may also include things such as maintenance grades and replacement insurance for damages or lost equipment. And you may be able to get mobile apps on a monthly pay as you go contracts

Improving cash flow, A mobile first approach can also have positive effects on your cash flow. Am mobile first approach can also have a positive effect on your cash flow. A mobile first approach enables you to use mobile invoicing and payment processing to greatly reduce the amount it takes to get paid.

## Improving Convenience and Customer Experience

No one likes to wait or be inconvenienced especially your customers. If you can improve your customers experience and provide more coinvent service that your than your competitors, customers are likely to give you their repeat business and also recommend you to the other people.

You can find many ways to improve customer experience. For example, consider how inconvenient it is for a customer to sit for hours waiting for a service call or delivery. By implementing a od mobile tracking solution you can narrow that time window. Customers appreciate knowing more precisely when to expect the service call or delivery.

# CHAPTER 17

## Your Business Online

Looking for the best website builder for small business? For small businesses on tight budgets, hiring a web designer or developer can be one expense too much. That's why website builder software is so important.

## Website builders:

Are a great option for small business owners with budget, skill and time constraints

Let you create an amazing website really fast at an affordable price

Allow you to use the money you would have spent on web development to grow your business

## How Do I Create a Professional Website for Free?

It is possible to create a website for free, but it may not look very professional.

When you look deeper, many free website builders aren't really free because:

You can't use your own domain

Your website is covered in ads you don't control

You have to pay for templates and any addons

You don't have full control over your site

Small Business Website Builders: What to Look For

## Here are a few of the most important factors to look for in website builders for small businesses.

Affordability:

One of the most important factors for small business owners is the price. You need a website builder that's affordable now and will still be affordable when your business grows. Think about how your site will evolve as your business grows.

The best website builder software will ideally include plans that allow you to scale up easily when you need to.

Ease of use: You'll also need your website builder to be easy to use and learn, with a wide range of templates for all situations. You should have a hassle-free way to add:

The basic website pages you need, such as the home page, about page, services page, and contact page

More complex features like image galleries and video content

Other website elements that some businesses need or want, like a blog, a booking or reservation system, membership features, or an online store

Search engine friendliness: You'll also want a website builder that's search engine-friendly, so your site content appears in search results for your **target keywords** and helps to attract your target customers.

# The Best Website Builder for Small Business.

Self-Hosted WordPress

Constant Contact Website Builder

 BigCommerce

Weebly

Member Press

Squarespace

Wix

## Step 0. Before Making a Small Business Website

Unlike the old days, building a small business website has become quite easy. You can do it all by yourself without knowing any coding or hiring a developer by following our step by step guide. Here is an overview of what you'll learn:

- Choosing a domain name for your small business website

- Purchasing website hosting

- Installing WordPress

- Making a content outline for your small business website

- Choosing a template to change your site's design

- Adding more features by using addons and extensions

- Resources to get help and improve your WordPress skills

## Step 1. What You Need to Make a Small Business Website

You will need the following three items to make a small business website.

- A domain name – This will be your website's name such as wpbeginner.com
- Website hosting – This will be your website's home and where all your files will be stored

- 60 minutes of your time

## Step 2. Setting up Your Small Business Website

There are two types of WordPress available. WordPress.com, which is a hosted solution, and then you have WordPress.org also known as self-hosted WordPress. We will be using self-hosted WordPress.org because it will give you instant access to all WordPress features out of the box.

Next, you will need a domain name and WordPress hosting to make a website.

## Step 3. Choosing a Domain Name for Your Small Business Website

**Tips on Finding a Domain Name for Your Business Website**

Domain names are crucial to the success of your website. You need to spend some time on choosing the perfect domain name for your business but don't overthink it.

1.

1. Stick to the .com version because users find it easier to remember (see .com vs .net – which is better)

2. Your domain name should be related to your business (For example, stargardening.com)

3. If your preferred domain name is not available, then try adding geographical location next to it. This increases your domain's visibility in local search results (For example, stargardeninghouston.com)

4. Keep it simple, short, and easy to pronounce.

## Step 4. Installing WordPress

After choosing your domain name, you will be asked to enter your account information such as name, address, email, etc.

Below that, you will see some extra hosting options that you can purchase. We don't recommend purchasing these extras right away, so go ahead and uncheck them. You can always add them later if needed.

## Step 5. Creating Content Layout for a Small Business Website

Now that you have WordPress installed, you need to create an outline of your website content. Good small business websites are simple and follow a standard website layout.

Simply go to **Pages » Add New** page to create a new page in WordPress.

**Here are some of the most common pages used in a small business website layout.**

1.

- **Homepage** – This is the welcome page of your website. Add your business name with a call to action to your services/products or contact page. Provide a brief description of why your customers should choose you.

- **About Us** – Your customers want to know more about people behind a business before they can make a decision. Create an about us page to tell users who you are, what are your business values, and what relevant experience you have in your industry.

- **Services / Products** – Create a page to list details about services or products you are offering. Add a heading for each service/product and provide a brief description. You can also add pricing or ask users to contact you for a quote.

* **Contact Us** – This is the page your users will need to contact you. You will need to add a contact form so that users can contact you directly. Additionally, you can add your businesses' physical address or phone number.

## 6. Choosing a Design for Your Website

By default, WordPress comes with a basic template that you can use. If you don't like the default theme, then there are thousands of free and paid WordPress themes that you can choose from.

# Your Business on Social Media

Social media and marketing may be one of your best tools to start with. Facebook, I started with my personal Facebook, but you want to setup a professional business page

Instagram, Twitter, Snapchat. business page with your business phone address number location and prices how to schedule to book or prices upcoming events, show cases and more about your business.

Social media has become the best free tool a start business can use. You can send invites and links to your current friends on product prices and service updates easier. And reach more potential customers. Now you also expose yourself to 24-hour access when running your business online via Face book and Instagram are you ready to sensor and be judge by your personal page.

**Social Media marketing,** or SMM, is a form of internet marketing that involves creating and sharing content on social media networks in order to achieve your marketing and branding goals. Social media marketing includes activities like posting text and image updates, videos, and other content that drives audience engagement, as well as paid social media advertising.

## SOCIAL MEDIA AND MARKETING: START WITH A PLAN

- What are you hoping to achieve through social media marketing?

- Who is your target audience?

- Where would your target audience hang out and how would they use social media?

- What message do you want to send to your audience with social media marketing?

### How Social Media Marketing Can Help You Meet Your Marketing Goals

Social media is a free and easy tool for businesses to connect directly with people interested in their brand, and it's fun (c'mon, we have gifs!). Free, easy, and fun doesn't mean that you can just log in and start posting, though. Before that, you need to set a social media strategy. Let me tell you why.

## Why your small business needs a social media STRATEGY?

Back in the day, with only a few options for social media, and before each social platform had been defined by its own specific value-add, businesses could just pop in and post whatever, whenever. The world of business on social media was sparse, and the capabilities of businesses to connect with their target audience even more so.

Not the case today, my friend.

Social media is now an important part of an inbound marketing strategy.

Creating valuable content and ranking well for it on the SERP is one thing but sharing that content out to the right people and getting those people that are interested in your brand, product, or service back to your site is another. And making sure that you're sharing the right content with the right people is also dependent on the platform. Each of the main social platforms popular now have a specific way they are used by consumers. Businesses, in turn, have begun to use each platform slightly differently to connect with their audiences.

In this guide, I'll take you through each platform and break down everything from what type of content you should post, how often you should be sharing, and best practices for each channel.

### We will be covering the main five social platforms:

Facebook

Twitter

LinkedIn

Instagram

YouTube

# Facebook marketing for small business

An organic post (of organic things) on Facebook

Facebook is one of the OG social media platforms. It has a massive user base with 1 billion daily and over 2 billion monthly active users. If your target customer is on any social media platform, it's likely Facebook. Bonus: Facebook also makes it easy to build target audiences for paid ad placements based on people who engage with your organic posts.

## WHAT TO POST

Facebook is a fairly conversational platform. However, if a consumer decides to like your Facebook page, they are likely looking to receive updates: they want to know about future sales and promotions, hear about new products, or get information about upcoming launches or events. It's important that you're connecting with those who follow you and providing the right type of content for them. Try sharing a few different types of content and seeing what resonates well with your audience by driving the most impressions, engagements, and shares. Once you've determined the types of content and updates your audience responds to, keep sharing in that way.

## Social media marketing can help with a number of goals, such as:

- **INCREASING WEBSITE TRAFFIC**
- Building conversions
- Raising brand awareness
- Creating a brand identity and positive brand association
- Improving communication and interaction with key audiences

The bigger and more engaged your audience is on social media networks, the easier it will be for you to achieve every other marketing goal on your list!

**Best Social Media Marketing Tips**

**Ready to get started with marketing on social media?** Here are a few social media marketing tips to kick off your social media campaigns.

**Social Media Content Planning** — As discussed previously, building a social media marketing plan is essential. Consider keyword research and competitive research to help brainstorm content ideas that will interest your target audience. What are other businesses in your industry doing to drive engagement on social media?

**Great Social Content** — Consistent with other areas of online marketing, content reigns supreme when it comes to social media marketing. Make sure you post regularly and offer truly valuable information that your ideal customers will find helpful and interesting. The content that you share on your social networks can include social media images, videos, info, graphics, how-to guides and more.

**A Consistent Brand Image** — Using social media for marketing enables your business to project your brand image across a variety of different social media platforms. While each platform has its own unique environment and voice, your business's core identity, whether it's friendly, fun, or trustworthy, should stay consistent.

• **Social Media for Content Promotion** — Social media marketing is a perfect channel for sharing your best site and blog content with readers. Once you build a loyal following on social media, you'll be able to post all your new content and make sure your readers can find new stuff right away. Plus, great blog content will help you build more followers.

It's a surprising way that content marketing and social media marketing benefit each other.

- **Sharing Curated Links** — While using social media for marketing is a great way to leverage your own unique, original content to gain followers, fans, and devotees, it's also an opportunity to link to outside articles as well.

**Tracking Competitors** — It's always important to keep an eye on competitors—they can provide valuable data for keyword research and other social media marketing insight. If your competitors are using a certain social media marketing channel or technique that seems to be working for them, considering doing the same thing, but do it better!

**Measuring Success with Analytics** — You can't determine the success of your social media marketing strategies without tracking data. Google Analytics can be used as a great social media marketing tool that will help you measure your most triumphant social media marketing techniques, as well as determine which strategies are better off abandoned.

**Social Media Crisis Management** — Things don't always go seemingly well for brands on social media. It's best to have a playbook in place so your employees know how to handle a snafu.

# CHAPTER 18

# Grow Your Business

If you run a small business, there's a good chance you have a strategy for growing that business. If you don't, then you will definitely want to start thinking about it, because things change quickly in the world of small enterprises. So, no matter your stage in concocting your growth plan, follow these steps to ensure success in execution. Branch out into new products and services. You have found your niche, and it works for you.

Many companies have long and successful tenures servicing a specific niche but find it incredibly difficult to achieve any significant growth without expansion into new products and services.

The fact is, selling only one, or a limited number of products or services can only take your business so far. So, you always need to have in mind what additional strings you want to add to your bow in regard to what your business offers.

I prerequisite characteristics will shake up the dynamic of your existing team. As long as it is done carefully, and in the confines of your company culture, then this will take your business to the next level.  As a small business owner, you are connected to your business in many ways that have the potential to make it very difficult to keep your personal life and business life separate. Although this is especially true for sole proprietors, it is also often the case with other (larger) small businesses. Your business, after all, is your baby and chances are you are much more emotionally invested in it than you even realize.

There are plenty of advantages that come from this dynamic -- you are passionate about your business  you work long hours and will do anything to get the job done, you are willing to make sacrifices for your work, you are loyal to your customers and clients. But there are also disadvantages – you rarely take breaks you tend to lose your objectivity when talking about business matters, you do it all in your business and often have difficultly delegating and letting go.

One other significant disadvantage, particularly for small business owners who are not sales savvy, is the need to be able to sell your products and services. And because you personally are so intertwined with your business, this means selling yourself. This makes many small business owners uncomfortable; it often feels unnatural. But if you are not advocating for yourself, you can't expect anyone else to do it for you.

The good news is there are ways to sell yourself by being proactive about exploring new opportunities, forging new relationships and positioning yourself in a positive light that eliminate any apprehensions you may have about sales. Here are a few ways to comfortably adopt a sales-driven mindset without feeling like you're selling out.

## 5 WAYS TO SALE AND INCREASE YOUR BUSINESS

1. **Use Client Testimonials or Case Studies:** You can make it easier for potential clients to see what you have to offer by compiling and offering testimonial from your happy clients. You can collect these words of praise and display

them on a page on your website, or you can provide them to potential clients on an individual basis. You can make these testimonials even more useable by creating case studies that drill deeper to your clients and how your products and services have helped them reach success. Keep in mind that client testimonials don't have to be formal letters of recommendation either. You can collect and ask for permission to use casual compliments and customer feedback as it comes in from clients. You can record audio or video testimonials, and even prepare a standard testimonial form for clients to complete at the end of a project to make it easier for them to provide feedback.

1. **Develop a Professional Website:** Your website is one of the best online promotional tools you can maintain for your business. Make the facts of your past successes accessible and easy to absorb for prospective clients. Include examples of past work, project case studies, and testimonials. You can also include client references, detailed information about your work process, and answers to frequently asked questions.

2. **Be Willing to Help Others:** Another way to establish your worth and sell your business is by being willing to share your expertise and help others. This can mean offering help to colleagues with challenges they are dealing with, promoting others through social media, and sharing tips, articles and other items of value for free.

1. **Provide a Guarantee:** One way to show your confidence in your business is to provide some sort of guarantee or warranty for your services. If you are a plumber, for example, you may consider providing a limited time warranty that will cover the work you do and some of the potential problems that may occur. You can even use this idea to create preventative service packages which you can sell to clients.
Depending on the type of business you have you can also provide a money-back guarantee for your services. You will want to make sure you clarify the terms of the guarantee to avoid any potential conflicts later on.

1. **Encourage Word of Mouth:** We all know the power of word of mouth marketing. Do your clients tell their own colleagues about the work you do and regularly make referrals? Don't be shy about asking your clients to

recommend you to others. You may even want to offer an incentive for referrals to encourage recommendations. And always say thank you to the introducer for any connections made.

These simple actions can help you sell your business more effectively without having to adopt harder hitting sales tactics that may make you uncomfortable. And the more you do these things, the easier it will be for you to be proactive about promoting yourself and your business.

# CHAPTER 19

# Doing Business in A Crisis

*7 GUIDELINES TO DOING BUSINESS WITH DIGNITY, INTEGRITY AND RESPECT DURING TIMES OF TRAGEDY*

**Be adaptable** it's one of the benefits of entrepreneurship. As I mentioned above, during each separate crisis that hit, we were in the middle of a major product or program launch. Pull off a major launch despite challenging conditions, we instead tweaked the whole plan to allow for a postponement. By being flexible and rolling with the punches a bit, we were able to demonstrate respect for those affected by the storm and we were also able to give our team the time that they needed to be with their own families as well.

**Turn off pre-scheduled online activity** During times of tragedy, it's important to be aware of any online activity— automated email promotions, tweets, face-book posts, blog updates, etc. that you've pre-scheduled. Allowing businesses-usual posts for your latest product or service to be sent out during a time when serious news is unfolding, can certainly appear disrespectful and insensitive. My advice is to cease all scheduled updates for the time being. It's just not relevant.

**Use your platform instead** to provide support and much-needed resources for any entrepreneur with a list of followers —large or small—and a social media presence, realize that you do have a platform. When you speak, people listen so it's ok to lead with your heart and intuition. Communicate your condolences, support—whatever is appropriate. Your voice of empathy may help others to feel better. Then offer resources.


**Be mindful of customers and clients in the affected areas** Determine if you have any customers or clients who are personally affected by the crisis. Then reach out. Is there a way you can help them? Help those who support you as a business. Loyalty goes a long way—and it works both ways.

**Avoid newsjacking. Newsjacking** is the practice of capitalizing on breaking news to promote your company's products or services. (Unless your company offers real-time relevant products or services that directly benefit those affected by the crisis, this is just not a good practice, and frankly it's out of integrity.

**Always err on the side of love,** authenticity and compassion in business, we're often focused on marketing strategy, competition and increased revenues. After all, we're in business to earn a profit, right? But when faced with a decision on what the "right" thing to do is, allow your heart to be your compass. The time is now, more than ever to bring our hearts and souls into our businesses.

**Create a crisis plan with your team.** Use these guidelines to create your own company crisis plan and incorporate it into your operations manual. Let's face it, when disaster strikes, we're not always thinking clearly. Having a plan with a full checklist of the many things to consider ensures that business is carried out appropriately—and with humanity. It makes good sense for our companies, our employees and our customers and clients. And in the long term, your prospects and customers will choose you over others, because you have heart and you cared.

## 5 Ways to Protect Your Business from Employee Theft

Here are some ways to do protect your company from

### #1 - ACT TO SAFEGUARD YOUR PROPERTY

*Restrict access* to keys, computer data, inventory, supplies, and merchandise. Create passwords and change them frequently. Although cash is the easiest to steal, losses to inventory and merchandise for sale can be huge if someone can get access.

Business identity theft, in particular, is a growing concern among employers.

### #2 - CREATE WRITTEN PROCEDURES - THEN FOLLOW THEM!

Your employees should know what to expect in their jobs. You can create an atmosphere of efficiency that will help you track all business transactions. For example:

- Number all documents and forms and keep track of their use.

- Make sure you have the proper documents to assure that you are paying a bill for the right amount and to the right person.
- Set up payroll procedures so that you have control of the final action. One business owner has her bookkeeper do payroll using a **payroll service**. But the owner reviews each payroll and clicks "send."

### #3 - KEEP TRACK OF INVENTORY

Remember there are two types of inventory. All businesses have an inventory of supplies, including office supplies, and businesses selling products have an inventory of products and component parts or materials.

Your inventory of supplies is vulnerable to pilferage (employees taking small items). While it might not seem like it's worth keeping track of, theft of small items can add up. For example, printer cartridges are extremely expensive.

Your product inventory should also be **tracked and counted** (inventoried). In particular, keep closer track of high-value items and document disposal of all obsolete, damaged, or low-selling merchandise.

## #4 - DIVIDE UP DUTIES BETWEEN EMPLOYEES AND MONITOR

The duties you should be most concerned about are those of the people who do your bookkeeping and who handle merchandise. Establish two-step processes and then divide the steps between two people. For example, the person who does your bank reconciliation should not be the person paying the bills. Or, the person who takes in merchandise for sale should not be the person who decides if an item should be scrapped, or who enters the sale of an item.

## #5 - PERIODICALLY REVIEW THEFT-PREVENTION MEASURES

It's not enough to put these actions in place. You and your top executives must take time every so often to review. Check to see that all the items on your list of concerns have been addressed. Set key measures to make sure "slippage" is within a reasonable range. For example, look at your inventory turnover rate this year as compared to the last few years to detect greater-than-average turnover.

Yes, all of these safeguards are time-consuming, and they may be costly. But they take far less time and cost less than losing money to employee theft and embezzlement.

# 10 TIPS FOR DEALING WITH CUSTOMERS

1. LISTEN TO CUSTOMERS

2. APOLOGIZE

3. TAKE THEM SERIOUSLY

4. STAY CALM

5. IDENTIFY AND ANTICIPATE NEEDS

6. SUGGEST SOLUTIONS

7. APPRECIATE THE POWER OF "YES"

8. ACKNOWLEDGE YOUR LIMITS

9. BE AVAILABLE

10. GET REGULAR FEEDBACK

## 1. Listen to Customers

Sometimes, customers just need to know that you're listening. If they're confused or have a problem, by lending a listening ear, you're showing that you care and that you're not dismissing them.

## 2. Apologize

When something goes wrong, apologize. It's amazing how calming the words "I'm sorry" can be. Don't engage in fault-finding or laying blame but let them know you're sorry they had a problem.

Deal with the problem immediately and let the customer know what you have done.

### 3. Take Them Seriously

Make customers feel important and appreciated. No matter how ridiculous a question may sound to you; it's important to the customer. If they feel like they're being laughed at, or spoken down to, they will not purchase anything. Customers can be very sensitive and will know whether or not you really care about them.

### 4. Stay Calm

Difficult as it is sometimes, it is important to stay calm. Your calming approach will help your customer stay calm too. They will feel like you're in control of the situation and that you can help solve their problem.

### 5. Identify and Anticipate Needs

Most customer needs are emotional rather than logical. The more you know your customers, the better you become at anticipating their needs. Communicate regularly so that you're aware of problems or upcoming needs.

### 6. Suggest Solutions

Have a menu of calming remedies which you and your employees can use. Whether it's purely a refund or return, or if it's coupons or a free service. By agreeing in advance, the scenarios where you will provide these remedies, and how much you're willing to spend, you will be able to speak calmer and more confidently when offering the solution.

## 7. Appreciate the Power of "Yes"

Always look for ways to help your customers. When they have a request (as long as it is reasonable) tell them that you can do it. Figure out how afterwards. Look for ways to make doing business with you easy. Always do what you say you're going to do.

## 8. Acknowledge Your Limits

Yes, is a powerful word but if you're unable to fulfil a request: know your limits. You can't be everything to everyone. If you don't think you can fulfil the request, help them find an alternate remedy. Whether that remedy is your business or another, they will appreciate the extra mile you went to help them and will recommend your business to their network.

## 9. Be Available

Customer service is no longer just about face-to-face contact and telephone. If you're working in an industry or marketplace where customers are constantly online, you need to amend your service delivery to incorporate that. It does not need to be a dedicated helpdesk Twitter handle, simply make sure you respond promptly and informatively to clients on your main business Facebook page or to your Twitter account.

## 10. Get Regular Feedback

Feedback is a great way to grow both your business and your skills. Provide ways for customers to give feedback, whether it's a follow up email or phone call, a suggestions box or something more fun and innovative.

# CHAPTER 20

## BUSINESS INSURANCE LIABILITIES

Commercial general liability insurance, also known as general liability insurance, provides coverage for your business against claims of bodily injury, associated medical costs and damage to property. Why do I need General Liability Insurance? We understand the risks your company faces and the importance of knowing your business is properly protected. Having general liability insurance coverage protects your business against third-party claims of bodily injury or damage to someone else's property. However, it does not protect your own personal property. This section explains what our business general liability insurance offers. You should consider general liability insurance coverage, also called commercial general liability insurance, if you or your employees: Interact with clients face to face

**What does General Liability Insurance cover?**

*What is covered?* Bodily Injury Damage to third party property Personal injury Advertising injury Electronic data liability Medical expenses Defense costs Actions of your full-time employees and temporary staff Supplemental payments

*What is not covered?* Your property Vehicles and boats Personal identifiable information Professional services Employee injury / workers' compensation Intent to injure Coverage outside policy period Known claims prior to start of policy

# CHAPTER 21

# Employees /Payroll

Payroll is something many business owners hate because it can be complex. However, if you have only a couple of employees, you may want to do it yourself rather than using a third party. This article is a step-by-step "minicourse" in payroll. Take special note of payroll and payroll tax due dates.

**Steps in the Payroll Process The major steps in the payroll process are:**

Preparation: Before you begin to hire employees, you will need to prepare for payroll calculation and processing and decide who will do all the payroll tasks.

Paying employees: When you have employees, you must set up a system to calculate their pay, write paychecks, and distribute them.

Post-payment: After you have paid employees, you must set aside money for taxes, complete a payroll register, make tax payments, and send payroll reports to the IRS at the correct times

# Before You Hire Employees

12-step checklist to make sure you complete all pre-employment tasks

1. Make decisions on how and when to pay employees, including:

   - Which employees will be hourly, and which will be salaried?

   - How often will you pay employees—weekly, twice a month, every other week, or monthly?

- How and when will you pay overtime?

- How will you require hourly employees to keep track of their time?

- What paid time off will you provide for hourly employees? You are not legally required to pay employees for any time off, but most businesses pay for holidays, vacations, sick days, or personal days.

Decide on an accounting system. Most small businesses use an online accounting system with a payroll processing option. You might also look into Android small business payroll apps and Square or Quick Books payroll online.

5. **Collect the paperwork needed for new hires to sign.**

Each new employee must complete certain paperwork as part of on boarding. You, as the employer, must be certain that the new hire forms and application are completed and filed. These forms include: • An IRS W-4 Form to designate withholding. • An application forms. • An I-9 Form to show eligibility to work in the United States. • State and local tax withholding election documents. Make Your Dream Business a Reality

6. **Set up a separate payroll bank account at your bank.**

This will be used for writing paychecks or paying through employee direct deposit and for depositing funds you collected from employees for federal and state income tax and for FICA taxes (Social Security and Medicare taxes) and other amounts. A separate payroll account can help you keep track of these transactions without having them mixed up with your general business bank account. federal (and state and local, if applicable) income taxes.

Write paychecks (or send them by direct deposit).

**Write paychecks and distribute them to the employees.**

Get totals for payroll tax deposits. When you are finished with the payroll, you will need to get totals for all employees for (a) gross pay, (b) federal, state, and local withholding, (c) FICA taxes, and (d) any other deductions.

You will need these amounts for payroll tax deposits and reports. After Paying Employees: Payroll Tax Deposits Depending on the size of your payroll, you must make payroll tax deposits to the IRS on a semi-weekly or monthly basis for:

• the amounts you withheld from employee pay for federal and state income taxes

- the amounts you deducted from employee pay for Social Security and Medicare

- Make payments for federal unemployment tax on a regular basis.

- Make payroll tax deposits to your state, and possibly your locality, in addition to federal payroll tax deposits. Payroll Tax Reporting Businesses are also required to submit payroll tax reports on a regular basis. You must do the following:

- Submit a quarterly report to the IRS on Form 941 showing the amount of your payroll tax liability and the amounts you have paid on this liability during the previous quarter.
- Submit an annual unemployment tax report on Form 940 to the IRS showing the amount of your unemployment tax liability and the amounts you have paid on this liability.

- Submit other state unemployment and workers' compensation reports.

**Create a Payroll Register To keep track of all payroll information for each employee, you will need to create and maintain a payroll register.**

Most online accounting systems have a payroll register as part of their package of reports but, just in case, here's the information on what to include in that document.

**You will need it for year-end payroll totals and reports.** Finally, create a Yearly Tax Calendar Creating and maintaining a month-by-month payroll tax calendar, either on your accounting/payroll software or manually, will help you keep track of all those payroll tax dates during the year. Add in your state's payroll tax dates for a complete calendar.

Sometimes, small businesses get in a rut. They don't step back and plan for the future or come up with creative ideas for improving the business. This chapter presents ten ideas that may work wonders for your business.

## Team Up with Another Company

Consider a joint venture or strategic alliance with another company. These ventures or alliances can be broad (such as a joint venture to develop a new product or technology) or simple (such as agreement to co-advertise a product or service). The most logical strategic partners are companies in related industries, but on occasion, you may want to include competitors in that list. **Strategic alliances offer the following benefits:**

Access to capital

Access to international markets

Access to new distribution channels

Access to new or existing products

Access to new technology

Enhanced ability to compete

Enhanced credibility

Reduced cost and uncertainty

# CHAPTER 22

# Get Advice

Because you can't possibly know everything you need to make your business successful, get advice from as many sources as you can. Talk to your lawyer, accountant, and banker. Ask questions of entrepreneurs who have survived some of the same problems that you face. If they're willing, your competitors can provide particularly valuable advice.

**7 Helpful Business Tips**

1. Build a Support Network

2. Be Very Specific with Your Goals

4. Keep Your Overhead Low

5. Find Your Best Niche—and Stick with It

6. Keep Your Day Job Just a Little Longer

7. Avoid Distractions at All Costs

**Who knows – you may end up in some kind of strategic alliance with them?**

One way to get systematic advice is to set up a Board of Advisors. Include people with different experience and backgrounds on your board. Have regular meetings (once a month or so) during which you bounce questions and ideas off board members.

People may be more willing to take on this task because it generally involves far less responsibility and liability than being on Board of Directors. (Make sure to give them some incentive for participating, such as stock options or a small fee.)

## Send Gifts to Your Key Customers

Successful businesses build up goodwill. If your company has some key customers, consider sending the main contact a present as a show of appreciation. This present doesn't have to be a Ferrari or a Picasso – just some small token that says you value their business. Just think how you would feel if one of your suppliers did that. Wouldn't you be more likely to give that supplier a preference in future dealings?

Consider giving the following items as gifts:

Desk clock

Gift certificate for two to a classy restaurant

Nice wine or champagne

Tickets to a hot show or sporting event

A gift tailored to the recipient's hobby

Seek Financing When You Don't Need it

If your business is doing well, you may – mistakenly – not see any pressing need to obtain more bank financing or equity funding. But the best time to seek financing is when you don't need it. You aren't forced into a corner and you don't risk cash-flow problems if you have adequate credit.

Consider going to a lender to establish a credit line and soliciting venture capitalists or other investors for an equity investment in your company, even if you don't need the financial boost right now. Banks and investors are more inclined to approve your business for loans when that business is doing well. And you're in a better bargaining position because you have absolutely no pressing need to obtain financing.

## Try Different Ideas

Successful businesses try a lot of different things – using different advertisements, adding new products, and improving old products. By trying new things, you can obtain increased flexibility and find better approaches to your business. Encourage new ideas from employees and customers. Don't be afraid to try out the new ideas, especially if the cost isn't outrageous. Who knows? Maybe your next idea will be the equivalent of the hula hoop, the semiconductor chip, or penicillin. Well, maybe not. But hopefully the next idea at least keeps you excited about the business.

Motivate and Reward Employees You absolutely have to reward and motivate employees to make your business successful. By failing to motivate and reward employees, you risk losing your best workers.

You can motivate and reward employees in many ways. Of course, raises, bonuses, and perks are always effective, but people also want to be recognized and encouraged for good performance. So, make sure that you continually recognize your employee's achievements.

For true motivation, consider including employees in a stock option or profit-sharing plan.

# Chapter 23

# Research Your Competition

You need information about your competitors to make good competitive decisions and to help you develop and market your products and services.

*So, start and continue to get as much information as you can about your competitors and their products. Information sources include the following:*

Advertisements

Annual reports

Customers who have bought from or been solicited by competitors

News clipping services

Newspaper and trade magazine articles

Product literature

The World Wide Web

*Review all the information that you can get and keep it in an organized file. It may come in handy late!*

## Get Favorable Publicity

Publicity or a favorable article about your company can generate some amazing results. Good publicity may generate new customers, interest potential investors in your company, and even raise your visibility to potential employees and strategic partners. Create some press releases that spotlight something interesting about your company or pitch a story to a local newspaper. Visibility can lead to great, unexpected rewards!

### 1. Create a Website with Valuable Contents

One of the very first ways to get your business online and in the eyes of the public is by developing a website for your business. This would help you share all your information along with the products and the services that you have to offer.

### 2. Have a Referral System

This is the best way in which you can gain publicity, but you would need to spend money for this. In short, you can just set up a referral system where a person can earn an amount of money when they refer your business or products to others.

Eventually, this would lead to a good amount of sales for your business. In short, you would have people marketing about your product as an affiliate, and they would be earning money just as you make both sales and cash through them

### 3. Video Marketing

Video marketing is another method that can help you to market your business via videos easily on platforms like YouTube. If you decide to use YouTube to make your video about your business, you are making the right choice. This is since YouTube is the third most visited site in the world and has about 50 million visitors that come here each day.

### 3. Guest Post on Authority or High-Profile Website

An authority website is a site where people usually begin to trust and regularly visit for a specific niche or topic. The website gets it popularity over time, with hard work and even by spending money on it. And by posting guest posts on such websites that are related to your niche, you would be able to make your site popular and get traffic on it.

### 4. Be Active on Social Networks

With the help of the social networks, you would be able to get free publicity of your business. For example; there are about 800 million visitors on Facebook alone, and this can help you get new members on your website.

All you need to do is spread the word by making a page, searching for groups and joining them. You can also create a group and invite people to connect easily. Keep updating bits on your website so that people will stick around. If you do not like Facebook, there are other places like Twitter, LinkedIn, and even Instagram.

**5. Offer Free Products Online**

In this method, it is obvious that you might need to give away free things to develop your fan group. You can do this on your social media page or even on your website. The free stuff can be anything from a product you are selling to eBooks, podcast, Webinar, etc., in exchange for emails or likes.

And with the help of the emails, you would be able to notify those people about new services or products. You can also extend this to develop relationships by sending emails to them

# Chapter 24

# People to Stay Away from When Starting Your Business

## 1. The Gossip

*"Great minds discuss ideas, average ones discuss events, and small minds discuss people." – Eleanor Roosevelt*

Gossipers derive pleasure from other people's misfortunes. It might be fun to peer into somebody else's personal or professional faux pas at first, but over time, it gets tiring, makes you feel gross, and hurts other people. There are too many positives out there and too much to learn from interesting people to waste your time talking about the misfortune of others.

## 2. The Temperamental

Some people have absolutely no control over their emotions. They will lash out at you and project their feelings onto you, all the while thinking that you're the one causing their malaise. Temperamental people are tough to dump from your life because their lack of control over their emotions makes you feel bad for them. When push comes to shove though, temperamental people will use you as their emotional toilet and should be avoided at all costs.

### 3. The Victim

Victims are tough to identify because you initially empathize with their problems. But as time passes, you begin to realize that their "time of need" is *all the time*. Victims actively push away any personal responsibility by making every speed bump they encounter into an uncrossable mountain. They don't see tough times as opportunities to learn and grow from; instead, they see them as an out. There's an old saying: "Pain is inevitable, but suffering is optional." It perfectly captures the toxicity of the victim, who chooses to suffer every time.

### 4. The Self-Absorbed

Self-absorbed people bring you down through the impassionate distance they maintain from other people. You can usually tell when you're hanging around self-absorbed people because you start to feel completely alone. This happens because as far as they're concerned, there's no point in having a real connection between them and anyone else. You're merely a tool used to build their self-esteem.

### 5. The Envious

To envious people, the grass is always greener somewhere else. Even when something great happens to envious people, they don't derive any satisfaction from it. This is because they measure their fortune against the world's when they should be deriving their satisfaction from within. And let's face it, there's *always* someone out there who's doing better if you look hard enough. Spending too much time around envious people is dangerous because they teach you to trivialize your own accomplishments.

### 6. The Manipulator

Manipulators suck time and energy out of your life under the façade of friendship. They can be tricky to deal with because they treat you like a friend. They know what you like, what makes you happy, and what you think is funny, but the difference is that they use this information as part of a hidden agenda. Manipulators always want something from you, and if you look back on your relationships with them, it's all taken, take, take, with little or no giving. They'll do anything to win you over just so they can work you over.

### 7. The Dementor

Dementors are evil creatures that suck people's souls out of their bodies, leaving them merely as shells of humans. Whenever a Dementor enters the room, it goes dark, people get cold, and they begin to recall their worst memories. based on highly negative people—the kind of people who have the ability to walk into a room and instantly suck the life out of it.

Dementors suck the life out of the room by imposing their negativity and pessimism upon everyone they encounter. Their viewpoints are always glass half empty, and they can inject fear and concern into even the most benign situations.

### 8. The Twisted

There are certain toxic people who have bad intentions, deriving deep satisfaction from the pain and misery of others. They are either out to hurt you, to make you feel bad, or to get something from you; otherwise, they have no interest in you. The only good thing about this type is that you can spot their intentions quickly, which makes it that much faster to get them out of your life.

### 9. The Judgmental

Judgmental people are quick to tell you exactly what is and isn't cool. They have a way of taking the thing you're most passionate about and making you feel terrible about it. Instead of appreciating and learning from people who are different from them, judgmental people look down on others. Judgmental people stifle your desire to be a passionate, expressive person, so you're best off cutting them out and being yourself.

### 10. The Arrogant

Arrogant people are a waste of your time because they see everything you do as a personal challenge. Arrogance is false confidence, and it always masks major insecurities. A University of Akron study found that arrogance is correlated with a slew of problems in the workplace. Arrogant people tend to be lower performers, more disagreeable, and have more cognitive problems than the average person.

## Seek business inspiration from your peers

Having a network of entrepreneurs and small business owners to talk to can be an invaluable support system. Not only can you give each other advice and feedback, it's also encouraging to hear that you're not alone in your challenges. Join small business owners' associations or meet ups and go to networking events to build your connections.

It's also helpful to read about successful entrepreneurs and hear about the challenges that they have faced while building their business. Some of the best small business success stories started with great challenges!

## REFLECT ON WHY YOU STARTED YOUR BUSINESS

The next time you're struggling to stay motivated in your business venture, step back and look at the big picture. Looking back at where you started from is a good way to remind yourself of how far along you have come and to measure how much you've already accomplished. Seek inspiration from your own small business success!

Thinking about why you started your business is an effective motivational strategy for many business owners Ask yourself—what motivated you to start the business in the first place? Getting back to the heart of why you started your business can help motivate you to keep going!

*"I was born for everything that I have in my heart."* -
*Mohammad Ali*

## Start-Up Checklist

Starting a new business is both exciting and rewarding but knowing where to begin can be a challenge.

Use our checklist below to help guide you through the key start-up tasks.

## Considering Starting-up

„ Find out whether you can work for yourself
„ Decide if you've got what it takes to be your own boss
„ Develop your business idea
„ Think about the money
„ Understand the different business types

## Business planning

„ Understand the importance of business planning „ Think about your financial planning
„ Develop your sales and marketing strategy
„ Plan to run your business

„ Create your business plan

## Premises

„ Rent or buy premises
„ Choose the right type of premises
„ Set up your business at home
„ Manage workplace health and safety

## Your customers

„ Learn how to describe your business to customers „ Understand your market
„ Build your brand
„ Get your pricing right

„ Sell your product or service „ Promote your business

## Help and Support

„ Find the right support for your new business „ Get tips on how to network
„ Find out about business mentoring

## Going for Growth

„ Work out if your business is ready to grow „ Take the next steps in your business journey

Get started with e-commerce

**Finance**

 Understand how much money you need to start-up

 Explore your finance options when starting-up
„ Decide if you need an accountant or an adviser
„ Understand how to set up a record-keeping system

„ Use your own money to start-up

„ Raise finance from family and friends
„ Raise finance from outside investors or other sources to get started „ Understand the basics of business banking
„ Find out what to do if you're refused finance
„ Meet your financial commitments

**Business Structures**

„ Choose the right business model and legal structure „ Register with Companies House
„ Name your business

**Business taxes**

„ Get to grips with business taxes
„ PAYE and payroll
„ Find out how PAYE works
„ Find out if you need to operate PAYE
„ Decide whether you need to register as an employer „ PAYE when taking on a new employee

„ Keep PAYE records
„ Set up a payroll system
„ Make PAYE payments to HMRC
„ Find out what to do for PAYE when an employee leaves

## Tax for the Self-employed

„ Get started with Income Tax and National Insurance
„ Get to grips with expenses and records if you're self-employed „ Find out about Self-Assessment and your tax return

## Corporation Tax

„ Get started with Corporation Tax

## Vat

„ Understand VAT invoices and receipts
„ Run and manage your VAT account
„ VAT registration: how to apply and when „ Get to grips with VAT and your business

**Insurance**

„ Protect your business and premises

**Trading with other countries**

„ Trade with other European Union countries
„ Trade with countries outside the European Union „
Trade with other countries using the internet
„ Find out about excise duty

**Employing people**

„ Take on staff

# Small Business Tax Checklist

**When you come in to see us at tax-time, please bring the following items to assist us in completing your tax return quickly.**

## Income

### Income from sales and / or the provision of services

- [ ] Bank statements indicating the nature of each deposit
- [ ] Reconciled cashbook including drawings taken from the business before banking
- [ ] Debtors listing
- [ ] QuickBooks/ MYOB files

### Banks, building societies, investments and term deposit accounts

- [ ] Bank statements with total interest received

### Rental properties

- [ ] Statements of rental income received

### Share trading statements

- [ ] Statements of shares purchased, sold or held (with price, dates purchased or sold, brokerage/stamp duty)
- [ ] Dividend statements

### Disposal of plant and property

- [ ] Dates and values of purchase and sale
- [ ] Provide asset description

### Capital Gains

- [ ] Details of any other personal or business assets acquired on or after 20/09/85 that were sold in the tax year.
- [ ] Details of additions/improvements to assets.

### Assessable Government & Other Payments

- [ ] Details of any assessable Government Industry Payments

### Other income

- [ ] Bank statements, receipts, invoices, cash book records of any other income

### Annual turnover

- [ ] Calculate annual turnover – provide details as necessary

## Expenses

### Loans

- [ ] Statements for all loans owing by the business, with an end of financial year balance and interest paid.

### Employees

- [ ] Copies of payment summaries and annual reconciliation for salaries and wages.
- [ ] Information relating to super contributions made for each employee and director.

### Rental Property

- [ ] Details of all expenditure incurred.
- [ ] Date of purchase of rental property as per contract.
- [ ] Rent paid by business.

### Motor vehicles (if used by business)

- [ ] Expenditure on fuel, oil, registration, repairs etc
- [ ] Log books
- [ ] Odometer readings for the first and last date of the financial year.
- [ ] Total business km for financial year
- [ ] Engine size

### Travel expenses

- [ ] Travel diary and other documentation

### Insurance

- [ ] Details of policy, provider, premiums, amount covered

### Assets

- [ ] List all business assets showing date of purchase, price, description, hire purchase or lease details.
- [ ] Details of any repairs or maintenance to business assets during the tax year.

### Leased plant and motor vehicles

- [ ] Detailed list of all plant and motor vehicles leased and expenses for each including contracts.

### Superannuation contributions

- [ ] Name of fund, policy number, contributions paid on behalf of each of the owners of the business.

### Other expenses

- [ ] Petty cash expenditure summary, expense items
- [ ] Documentation of other items you think might be deductible – cheque butts, receipts.

# Social Media Checklist

BUFFER

**Check Before You Publish**

A social media checklist to make sure you're delivering the most valuable, actionable, engaging social media messages for your audience!

- [ ] Is it educational or entertaining?
- [ ] Is the voice correct?
- [ ] Is it too long?
- [ ] Is the URL correct?
- [ ] Should I target a specific audience?
- [ ] Did I use the right keywords and hashtags?
- [ ] How many times have I already posted today?
- [ ] Did I spell check?
- [ ] Will I be okay with absolutely anyone seeing this?
- [ ] Is this a reactive post or is it well thought-out?
- [ ] Did I make the most of visual content?
- [ ] Did I make the most of my update text?

**[Business Name]**                                    # Business Startup Costs

| FUNDING | | Estimated | Actual | Under (Over) |
|---|---|---|---|---|
| Investor Funding | | | | |
| Owner 1 | | 10,000 | 9,600 | 400 |
| Owner 2 | | 5,000 | 5,500 | (500) |
| Other | | | | - |
| | Total Investment | 15,000 | 15,100 | (100) |
| | | | | |
| Loans | | | | |
| Bank Loan 1 | | | | - |
| Bank Loan 2 | | | | - |
| Non Bank Loan 1 | | | | - |
| | Total Loans | - | - | - |
| Other Funding | | | | |
| Grant 1 | | | | - |
| Other | | | | - |
| | Total Other Funding | - | - | - |
| **Total FUNDING** | | **15,000** | **15,100** | **(100)** |

| COSTS | | Estimated | Actual | Under (Over) |
|---|---|---|---|---|
| Fixed Costs | | | | |
| Advertising for Opening | | | | - |
| Basic Website | | | | - |
| Brand Development | | | | - |
| Building Down Payment | | | | - |
| Building Improvements/Remodeling | | | | - |
| Tools & Supplies | | | | - |
| Travel | | | | - |
| Truck & Vehicle | | | | - |
| Other 1 (specify) | | | | - |
| Other 2 (specify) | | | | - |
| | Total Fixed Costs | - | - | - |
| | | | | |
| Average Monthly Costs | | | | |
| Advertising (print, broadcast and internet) | | | | - |
| Business Insurance | | | | - |
| Business Vehicle Insurance | | | | - |
| Employee Salaries and Commissions | | | | - |
| Supplies | | | | |
| Telephone | | 63 | 65 | (2) |
| Travel | | | | - |
| Public Utilities | | | | - |
| Website Hosting/Maintenance | | 24 | 15 | 9 |
| Other 1 (specify) | | | | - |
| Other 2 (specify) | | | | - |
| | Total Average Monthly Costs | 87 | 80 | 7 |
| | x Number of Months | 6 | | |
| | Total Monthly Costs | 522 | 480 | 42 |
| **Total COSTS** | | **522** | **480** | **42** |
| **SURPLUS (DEFICIT)** | | **14,478** | **14,620** | **(142)** |

## SMALL BUSINESS LOAN APPLICATION

### CHECK LIST

This checklist has been provided to assist you through the process of gathering the information for the initial evaluation of your loan request. Complete information will be necessary to process your application. All forms are provided herein unless otherwise noted:

1. **Loan Request Form**

2. **Personal Financial Statement** -- Complete on all owners, directors, guarantors, and stockholders with 20% or more of total stock issued. (Copy form as needed.)

3. **Management Resume** -- provide complete resumes on all individuals referred in #2 above. (Copy form as needed.)

4. History of Business Form

5. Estimated Project Costs

6. Certification and permission to obtain personal credit reports.

IN ADDITION, PROVIDE THE FOLLOWING:

7. Business Indebtedness Worksheet

8. Three Years Projections of Profit & Loss (Use enclosed form as a guide).

9. Interim Business Financial Statement - must be less than 60 days old.

10. Business Financial Statements and Tax Returns - Income statements, balance sheets, and time periods. tax returns for the three prior year-end

11. Accounts Receivable and Accounts Payable Aging Schedules - as of the same date as the income statement and balance sheet (if applicable).

12. Business Purchase Agreement (if applicable).

13. Historical Financial Information on the Business Being Acquired (if applicable)

14. Uniform Franchise Offering Circular (if applicable).

15. Executed Franchise Agreement or Letter of Approval from Franchisor (if applicable).

16. Construction Quote or Real Estate Purchase Contract for New Building or Expansion (if applicable).

# PROFIT & LOSS PROJECTIONS

Applicant's Name _____

| | YEAR #1 | | YEAR #2 | | YEAR #3 | |
|---|---|---|---|---|---|---|
| | $ | % | $ | % | $ | % |
| **($000'S)** | | | | | | |
| **INCOME** | | | | | | |
| Gross Receipts | | | | | | |
| Cost of Goods Sold | | | | | | |
| **GROSS PROFIT** | | | | | | |
| | | | | | | |
| **EXPENSES** | | | | | | |
| Officer Salaries | | | | | | |
| (if a corporation) | | | | | | |
| Employee Wages | | | | | | |
| Accounting & Legal Fees | | | | | | |
| Advertising | | | | | | |
| Rent | | | | | | |
| Depreciation | | | | | | |
| Supplies | | | | | | |
| Electricity | | | | | | |
| Telephone | | | | | | |
| Interest | | | | | | |
| Repairs | | | | | | |
| Taxes | | | | | | |
| Insurance | | | | | | |
| Bad Debts | | | | | | |
| Miscellaneous | | | | | | |
| Other (explain) | | | | | | |
| | | | | | | |
| | | | | | | |
| **TOTAL EXPENSES** | | | | | | |
| **NET PROFIT BEFORE TAXES** | | | | | | |
| **LESS: INCOME TAXES** | | | | | | |
| **NET PROFIT AFTER TAXES** | | | | | | |
| **LESS: WITHDRAWALS** (if proprietorship or partnership) | | | | | | |
| **REMAINING NET PROFIT FOR LOAN REPAYMENT** | | | | | | |

Note: please attach assumptions upon which the income and expenses were calculated.

I Certify the foregoing data represents the potential annual earnings , to the best of my knowledge.

_____     _____     _____
SIGNATURE                         TITLE                  DATE

# Business Credit Application

To Obtain Credit With:
Dynamic Distribution Ltd. 208 – 39th Ave. NE Calgary AB T2E 2M5 (The Creditor)

Incorporated Name of Company Seeking Credit:

Trade Name of Company Seeking Credit

Director's Name(s):

Mailing Address:                                                Phone#:

Business Location if Different:

Type of Goods or Services Your Company Provides:

Bank:                          Branch:                          How Many Years?

Year and Make of Vehicle:                    Plate#:                Owned /
Leased?

Credit References: 1)                              2)

3)                              4)

**Certificate:**
I Certify the above information to be accurate and complete and hereby authorize the disclosure and release of any credit related information about myself to the Creditor.

Date:————— Print Name:————————— Sign Name:—————————

**Credit Terms:**
The Creditor will extend credit to the above listed company (Called "Your company") under the following terms:
Credit Limit:_____ Invoices Payable: 14 days
The Creditor is entitled to charge 2% per month (24% per annum) on any outstanding monies owed by your company.

# QuickBooks Setup Checklist

**Company information needed:**
- ☐ Company legal name and address
- ☐ Federal EIN or social security number
- ☐ State employer ID number
- ☐ Fiscal year end
- ☐ QuickBooks start date
- ☐ Type of business
- ☐ Income tax form used
- ☐ Accounting basis (cash or accrual)

**Chart of Account information needed:**
- ☐ Names and numbers (if used) for the chart of accounts
- ☐ Financial statements from the end of the previous tax year
- ☐ Trial balances on the start date
- ☐ Bank account numbers and balances
- ☐ Credit card numbers and balances
- ☐ Loan account numbers and balances
- ☐ Line of credit numbers and balances
- ☐ Value of assets
- ☐ Equity information (owner/stockholder contributions)
- ☐ Retained earnings for each year of operation

**Customer information needed:**
- ☐ Information for each customer: name/address/taxable status/etc.
- ☐ Customer payment terms
- ☐ Customer shipping methods
- ☐ Customer types
- ☐ Open balances/outstanding invoices as of start date

**Vendor information needed:**
- ☐ Information for each vendor: name/address/contact info/account number
- ☐ List of 1099 vendors and their tax ID numbers
- ☐ Vendor payment terms
- ☐ Shipping methods
- ☐ Vendor types
- ☐ List of outstanding bills as of start date

**Item information needed:**
- ☐ List of all service, inventory, non-inventory items
- ☐ Price list for items
- ☐ Inventory and inventory assembly numbering scheme
- ☐ Quantity/value of inventory on hand
- ☐ Reorder points for all inventory items
- ☐ Taxable status for items
- ☐ List of states in which the company must collect and pay sales tax
- ☐ Sales tax rates/agencies/liability amount as of start date
- ☐ Frequency of sales tax reporting
- ☐ Sales tax calculation basis (cash or accrual)
- ☐ Type of sales (wholesale, retail, etc.)

**Employee information needed:**
- ☐ Information for each employee: names, addresses, telephone numbers, SSN, etc.

**Payroll setup information needed:**
- ☐ Determine 941 deposits (monthly or by pay period), state withholding, local withholding, and unemployment tax (FUTA, SUTA)
- ☐ YTD information for each employee as of the payroll start date
- ☐ Earnings, additions, and deductions (payroll items) for payroll processing (401(k), reported tips, etc.)
- ☐ Employer federal, state, and local tax ID numbers
- ☐ YTD payroll liability payments

## Client Info Sheet & Contact Details   YOUR COMPANY NAME/LOGO

Note: All personal information is held securely in accordance with the appropriate legislation, confidential and treated appropriately.

### Client Information

Mr/Mrs/Miss/Ms/Other _____   Last name _____

Name you like to be called _____

Address _____

_____

### Telephone Numbers/Contact Details

Home _____   Work _____

Cellphone _____   Skype Id _____

Email/s _____

Best Contact Method/s (usual) _____

Best Contact Method/s (short notice) _____

### Employment Information

Occupation _____

Employer Name _____

### Personal Information

Date of Birth _____   Marital Status _____

Significant Other's Name _____

Significant Dates (eg. Wedding anniversary) _____

_____

No. of Children _____

Name(s) and Age(s) of Child(ren) _____

"Stay true to yourself, yet always be open to learn. Work hard, and never give up on your dreams, even when nobody else believes they can come true but you. These are not clichés but real tools you need no matter what you do in life to stay focused on your path."


Phillip Sweet

For more Information
Visit us online at
www.MindYaOwnBiz.com

Made in the USA
Columbia, SC
06 September 2019